PLATO TO-DAY

By G. Lowes Dickinson

PLATO AND HIS DIALOGUES
Second Impression

AFTER TWO THOUSAND YEARS
A DIALOGUE BETWEEN PLATO AND
A MODERN YOUNG MAN
Second Impression

**THE CONTRIBUTION OF ANCIENT GREECE
TO MODERN LIFE**

By Constantine Ritter

**THE ESSENCE OF
PLATO'S PHILOSOPHY**

PLATO TO-DAY

by

R. H. S. CROSSMAN

FELLOW AND TUTOR OF NEW COLLEGE, OXFORD

LONDON

GEORGE ALLEN AND UNWIN LTD

FIRST PUBLISHED IN 1937

CONTENTS

CHAPTER   PAGE

INTRODUCTION   9

1. PLATO AND THE MODERN WORLD   15

2. THE HISTORICAL BACKGROUND   23

3. SOCRATES   48

4. PLATO   95

5. PLATO LOOKS AT BRITISH DEMOCRACY   134

6. PLATO LOOKS AT BRITISH EDUCATION   155

7. PLATO LOOKS AT THE FAMILY   180

8. PLATO LOOKS AT COMMUNISM   204

9. PLATO LOOKS AT FASCISM   228

10. WHY PLATO FAILED   248

11. THE MODERN PLATO ONCE MORE   279

12. EPILOGUE   290

BIBLIOGRAPHY   301

INTRODUCTION

EVERY introduction is an apology, and this is no exception. *Plato To-day* needs a double apology, both to those listeners who liked the series "If Plato Lived Again" and to the B.B.C., who enabled me to give it.

For this book was supposed to be a reprint of the series, and when I sat down this summer to the task of editing the talks for publication, I fully intended to limit my activity to the tidying up of the scripts. So I cut the talks very carefully out of the *Listener*, and—since the paper on which the *Listener* is printed runs into blots if you try to write on it—I was compelled to paste the articles on to sheets of typing paper before correcting them.

There is nothing more gloomy than the prospect of a wireless talk presented in this form. The fish which swam, as I fondly believed, with some elegance upon the aerial waves, had been hauled out of its proper element and now lay gasping and mawkish in the arid wastes of printed matter. Any colour it may have possessed as a talk had vanished; instead, it had become a verbose, rambling and indecently intimate article. I began to realize why wireless talks are frowned upon by influential critics. Such people do not listen in, but they do read the *Listener*; and they therefore judge—and condemn—talks which they have read and never heard.

A good half-hour talk on a controversial subject must transgress every canon of literary form. Because of the listener who switches on half-way through and then writes to complain of the propaganda which the B.B.C. puts across, a talk cannot have one beginning, one middle, and one end, but must triplicate all three and judiciously mix them. Because of the listener who has to go away for five minutes in the middle, it must be content to take one or two main points and elaborate variations upon them, so that he can still understand, although he has missed one part of the argument. Because of the humourless listener there can be no irony or sarcasm, and each view discussed must be carefully labelled so that no one can mistake it for an official pronouncement of the B.B.C. Vigour and vividness, the lively contrast of conflicting opinions, the allusive sidelight on current affairs—all must be sacrificed, if need be, to avoid that bugbear of the B.B.C., "possible misunderstandings leading to correspondence."

But there are other difficulties which make the composition of a wireless talk on controversial subjects still more laborious. The artless lecturer who believes that his job is to state the truth—or his view of it, or Plato's view of it—simply and objectively, is quickly disillusioned. Objective truth, simply stated, is liable to horrible misinterpretation, if not by the British listener, then by some foreign power. To be broadcast, truth must be robed in the formless garments of guarded and impersonal qualification, which will render it innocuous to sensitive listeners of every political colour. The broadcast talk must be so well-balanced that no unbalanced Tory or Anarchist can take offence.

It is something of a feat to make talks written

under those conditions palatable to any intelligent mind. But since the conditions are official, it is best to accept them as obstacles to be circumvented. Once this is done, the composition of talks becomes an absorbing pursuit, an obstacle race in which the prize is forgotten in the delight of lighting a candle in a high wind while balancing an apple on your nose. I enjoyed it immensely and must express my thanks to the B.B.C. officials who trained me for it. Without Mr. Wilson and Mr. Luker I cannot conceive what I should have done. They not only showed me the course and pointed out the obstacles, but exposed their own persons to the high wind of criticism in order to shield my guttering candle. Any success the series may have had is due to them, and to Mr. Charles Morris, who both collaborated in it and did his best to eradicate the later blemishes of this book itself.

In preparing a series on Plato we were faced with one peculiar difficulty. Our intention was to show what Plato would think of the modern world. Now Plato was a truthful and a controversial thinker who had never faced the problems of wireless talks, and so when we began to vest him in broadcast robes, we found him extremely reluctant to wear this outlandish garb. Try as we might, he eluded our censorship, and started casting aspersions on respected prejudices and institutions. We could not induce him to qualify all his remarks and to try to please all tastes. He was always catching us out, and coming alive in a highly improper manner, and we regretfully began to realize that Plato would never become

a sound and reliable broadcaster. Any self-respecting
B.B.C. would have to give him up as hopelessly
partisan.

Plato *was* controversial and aroused the interest of
a good many listeners, but we were compelled to
leave out a good deal which he would have said.
When, therefore, I read again those gloomy scripts in
the *Listener*, it occurred to me that it might be worth
while to write a book in which, unhampered by the
limitations of broadcasting, I should try to describe
the attitude of Plato to our modern world. *Plato
To-day* is the result. Obviously it bears very little
resemblance to the talks series, and the B.B.C. is in no
sense responsible for it. Broadcast Plato must differ
profoundly from the written version, and for the
latter I am solely to blame. Those who found the
talks to their taste are warned that this book may
well be a sad disappointment, lacking in those
qualities of judicious indecision which the talks possessed. To all such readers I offer my apologies and
can only say that I believe that I have given here a
fuller portrait of Plato than I was able to give upon
the air.

In conclusion I should like to express my gratitude
to Mr. H. W. B. Joseph for his helpful criticism, to
Mrs. H. A. L. Fisher for reading through the proofs,
and to Zita Baker for typing and retyping the drafts
of the manuscript and also for many useful suggestions. My thanks are also due to Mr. W. B. Yeats
for permitting me to quote his poem "The Second
Coming" on page 226; and to the Master of Balliol,
whose translation of the *Republic* I have sometimes

cited. Where no reference is given the translations from the Greek have been specially made for this book.

R. H. S. C.

New College
  October 1936

PLATO TO-DAY

1 PLATO AND THE MODERN WORLD

PLATO was born in 427 B.C., just about two thousand three hundred and fifty years ago. He lived most of his life in a tiny city-state in Greece, and busied himself with the problems of his fellow Greeks, a people living in scattered cities around the Mediterranean and the Black Sea. In all that he tried to do for the Greeks he failed. Why then should people in this modern world bother to read what he had to say? Can it be worth while to go to a Greek thinker for advice upon the problems of an age so utterly different from his own?

To anyone who is not so steeped in the classical tradition that he finds all things Greek or Roman better than all things modern, these questions will seem extremely pertinent. The Greeks lived in small cities: we live in large nation-states. The Greeks depended on slave labour: we have abolished slavery. Greek religion was a tangle of superstition and philosophy: we, in the modern world, have the lesson of Christianity and have learnt from it a humanity and ideal of love and tolerance totally foreign to Greek thought. Admitted they were a gifted people who produced great literature, great architecture, and great sculpture, yet in the realm of science they showed a dilettantism and lack of interest which must seem repulsive to modern man, who has learnt by scientific method and patient perseverance to master that nature which the Greeks feared. We can enjoy Greek art and Greek literature: we may even enjoy Plato as an artist, but why should we bother ourselves to study Plato's views on politics and morality unless we happen to be interested in the byways of history? Plato is dead; why recall him to life instead of trying to solve the actual political and social problems of our own world? Why not set out ourselves, fearless and independent of all authority, to solve them in our own way by the light of our own native reason?

But can we? Is our modern reason, our modern outlook, so independent of the past? If social science has taught us anything, it is this—that man is not a "completely free intelligence," but, in large part at least, a product of his environment, conditioned in his feelings, his thoughts, his actions, by the society in which he lives. And the society in which he lives is itself a product of the historical process, not a pattern of life designed and constructed by rational minds. We are, in fact, creatures of history, and the story of the human race has been the story of our struggle to become, not the creatures, but the creators of history.

The contribution of modern science to this struggle has been the fashioning of a weapon with which man can free himself from the domination of nature. Distance, disease, starvation, are the tyrants which he can conquer by the aid of science, but even to-day science can tell us little about ourselves, or about the way in which we can build a decent and secure community. The scientist himself who, as Bacon put it, can control nature by discovering and obeying her laws, is still as a person the product of the society he lives in. In his own family and citizen life he is often the slave of the past, blindly submissive to the traditions of his country, his school, and his family. If we consider the *purposes* for which science is used, we shall see that by freeing himself from the domination of nature man has only accomplished half the task which his destiny has set him. The greater the knowledge of nature and the power over nature that he possesses, the larger the size of the state, the closer the communications between the continents of the world, the more dangerous becomes the subservience of man to tradition, and the refusal to ask himself the purpose, and the place of the society in which he lives.

But it was precisely this problem with which the Greeks were chiefly concerned. Experimental methods in the natural sciences were almost unknown in Greece, where men were busied with *social and political experiment*, with the attempt by the light of reason, or by trial and error, to devise a way of life, or, as we should call it, a social system. Greek civilization was, in fact, a laboratory of social science, and it was precisely its experimental nature which made it so impermanent, so ruthless, and so alive. The science of self-government both in the individual and in the community was the central interest of Greek culture.

The very smallness of the Greek city-state made it specially suitable for such social experiments. Where few lives are concerned, great risks can be taken.

Revolution in Greece was not the terrible responsibility which it has become in modern nation-states. A Greek city could go off the gold standard without creating a Greek crisis, far less a world crisis. It could experiment with countless types of constitutional and legal systems without profoundly disturbing its neighbours. And very largely for this reason, the Greeks were the first people to work out systems of social organization which we call constitutional governments. The experiments which the Greeks tried out on themselves in the laboratory of the city-state are still, hundreds of years after those city-states perished, the basis upon which we try to build our states in modern Europe. The application of *Reason* to the problems of morality and politics was their invention and their legacy to us. Under their hands *tabu* became law, government became not a privilege but a science, religion not a superstition but a creed. They left their rivers unbridged, their towns undrained, but they tried to make the life of man in society as clear and reasonable as the sculptures in which they portrayed him.

For the last hundred years, Western European man has been so busy conquering nature that he has left the development of society to the chances of a historical process which he has called (over-optimistically perhaps) by the name of *Progress*. This development has been as chaotic as it has been rapid. Thought about it has been concerned more to apologize for it after it has happened than to predict or plan its advance. The wild disarray of our world-society is in strange contrast to the meticulous neatness of the discoveries of science. In the latter there is co-operation and a systematic advance in all fields: in the former there are wars, conflicts, and rumours of final catastrophe.

Perhaps, after all, the contrast made earlier between Greek and modern life is not so great as it at first appeared. These scattered sovereign cities, largely dependent on imports for food supplies, filled with the jangle of party conflict and the threat of class-war, were like a small-scale map of modern Europe. The problems of government which harassed their rulers, the rules of diplomacy and the technique of propaganda they employed, have an astonishing similarity to their modern analogues. And so, naturally enough, the two fundamental problems of Greek city life, how to give freedom to the citizen without producing anarchy, and how to retain the independence of the sovereign state without falling under the constant threat of international war, are the fundamental problems of the modern world. Why did the Greeks fail to solve both of these problems?

If we raise this question, there is one man above all to whom we must turn. Plato's life was lived in the decline of the city-state. The grandeur of the defeat of Persia had paled long before he was born. More than all his contemporaries he felt the failure of Hellenism, and his diagnosis of that failure is the most ruthless, and the most objective which we possess. He lived, as we do, at the end of an epoch of expansion: he was twenty-five when the great war between Athens and Sparta ended in the defeat and humiliation of his countrymen; the Athenian Empire crumpled before his eyes, and he saw that the real task was not to rebuild Athens but to save Greece. To do that a searching analysis of the city-state and of the nature of man was necessary, for he saw that a "League of Cities" could only be constructed if the cities were fundamentally changed. To that task he devoted his life.

Thus in turning back to the world of Ancient History, we shall not be neglecting our own problems. On the contrary, to see those problems in miniature as they were first presented, is to see them *isolated* from a host of incidentals and accessories which blind and befog us when we look at the modern world. It is the peculiar skill of the scientist to isolate the phenomena he wishes to examine, and it is the peculiar difficulty of the social scientist that he can never get society into a laboratory, or dissect human relations under a microscope. The study of Greek politics offers a sort of substitute for this isolation and abstraction to which modern problems can rarely be submitted, and the study of Plato is the first step in this study of Greece.

If we consider Plato's life we shall see why this is so.

The analysis of a society can rarely be made at the moment when that society is most creative and vital. Reflection and criticism arise only when the rifts begin to show and conflicts refuse to be resolved in action. Philosophy is thus the outcome of failure: we do not analyse the best till it is past. Then we attempt to recall a golden age, or to reconstruct a broken society in the pattern of that age. In Greece, as in our own day, the age of expansion was an age of activity: theory and analysis began when that expansion ceased, and it became clear that planning, reconstruction, and self-restraint were necessary if collapse was to be averted.

It is this striking similarity between the age of Plato and our own which makes him so apposite a study for the post-war world. It is no exaggeration to say that the World War of 1914 has made Plato intelligible to us. For us, too, the old traditions are breaking down; art has lost touch with the life of the people, democracy is in danger. We, too, are standing on the edge of the abyss, and philosophy has become a matter of life and death instead of a matter for polite discussion. Our life has become "politicized": we are forced to make up our minds if we are Democrats or Marxists or Fascists.

Is the equality of man a mere idle dream? Is the freedom of the spirit worth the bother it gives, or the preservation of national sovereignty worth the perils it brings? These are no longer merely questions to discuss; they are political issues, the expressions of conflicts on whose solution depends the future of our civilization. We can no longer solve them at our convenience by armchair discussion: they must be solved by action at any moment when the conflict becomes acute.

These are the signs of a transitional epoch, and it is not surprising to find that once again men's minds have been turned to Plato, the philosopher of transition. For many decades the philosopher has been regarded as an "academic," a dreamer or thinker, remote from the petty conflicts of the everyday world: and Plato has inevitably been portrayed as a philosopher of this kind. Now, when our civilization has reached a crisis similar to that in which he lived, we are able to see him as he really was—an idealist, thwarted in action, a revolutionary reformer who could find no political basis for his reforms.

2 THE HISTORICAL BACKGROUND

IF the argument of the preceding chapter is correct, it is clearly impossible to give a simple answer to the question, "If Plato lived again, what would he think of the modern world?" For Plato was no disembodied spirit hovering with objective gaze over the process of history: he was a Greek, an Athenian, and an aristocrat who lived a troubled life in the fifth and fourth centuries before Christ. Before we can bring him back to our world we must learn to know him in his own, and for this reason we must pause for a moment to glance at the history of Greek civilization and to pick out some of its distinctive characteristics.

Greek civilization was not confined to the country we call Greece, or even centred there. All round the Mediterranean, from the Straits of Gibraltar to the Syrian coast, up the Dardanelles, on the Sea of Marmora, and round the whole of the Black Sea, were scattered the independent Greek cities. Not only the coasts of the mainland but the islands too were occupied; in particular Sicily, Crete, Cyprus, and the Greek Cyclades. Only where the Carthaginians held control in the Western Mediterranean were the Greeks repulsed in their colonizing activities. These colonies were quite unlike any modern colonies. The colonists, in spite of the ties of blood and commerce which often bound them to the mother city, were citizens of independent cities and, generally speaking, lived on equal terms with the "barbarians" around them. Thus the modern notion of the nation-state, with its coloured empire and imperial rivalries, was completely foreign to the Greek mind. The Greek recognized his nationality only in the sense that he felt himself a *Hellene*, culturally distinct from the peoples with whom he came into contact. But the idea that cultural unity should imply a common government or that cultural superiority gave the right to political domination was fundamentally un-Greek.

A Hellenic state was envisaged by none save empty dreamers, a federation of Hellenic city-states only by a few bold statesmen, who foresaw that the internecine rivalries of the politicians must ultimately exhaust the energy of their peoples. For the ordinary Greek citizen the city-state seemed to be as obvious a unit of political life, and as essential to security and freedom, as the nation-state appears to the ordinary European. Equally foreign was the modern notion of colonization and empire. The imperial control of foreign peoples, whether for their exploitation or for their well-being, did not appeal to a merchant people content to trade and live on equal terms with all. The Greek did not feel the weight of "the white man's burden," or at least did not feel that Greek culture could be imposed by the political and military control of vast continents. Alexander, the imperial missionary of Hellenism, was a Macedonian, not a Greek.

It is idle to search for a single cause of this remarkable difference between Greek civilization and our own. Geography doubtless played its part: for political unity between the townships scattered round the mountainous shores of the Aegean was difficult to achieve. But more important still is the simple fact that life in a tiny city-state contrasted so favourably with anything to be found in any of the great Oriental empires. The Greek international anarchy (for such it must be called) may have been the final cause of the collapse of Greek independence: it was also the chief reason for the wellnigh incredible activity which the Greeks displayed from about 750 B.C. until, in about 350 B.C., the rise of the Macedonian Empire brought the end of the "Classical Period." When we remember this we shall understand the reluctance of Greeks as farsighted as Plato or Aristotle to face the possibility that the city-state had played its part and must be replaced by new forms of political organization.

The earliest period of Greek life of which we know enough to write any connected history is the early eighth century B.C. By this time the Greeks were settled in Greece proper and along the coast of Asia Minor. Homer had become a mythical figure; Mycenae, the city of Agamemnon, a ruin crumbling into the earth. The age of migrations was over, and it was already difficult to distinguish the newcomers from the original population. After the dark ages of confusion in which the Cretan civilization had foundered, the new era dawns with a burst of colonial expansion by a number of Greek cities. Between 750 and 500 B.C., colonists from Corinth and Miletus and many other towns occupied many of the best available sites on the coastlines of the Mediterranean and Black Sea:

hundreds of new cities sprang up and Greek life as we know it began.

What is the explanation of Greek colonization? Partly, no doubt, it was caused by the pressure of population in countries whose agricultural possibilities were strictly limited by the climate and the poverty of the soil: partly by the fact that the inland territories of Asia Minor were already occupied while in Greece proper there is hardly any inland territory which is not mountain or desert. But though land-hunger may have been *a* cause, undoubtedly trade was another. The Greeks were always a maritime people, and already in the Dark Ages Greek traders were active. Naturally enough, therefore, when expansion was necessary, it followed the trade-routes. Not only the hungry peasant, but the ambitious merchant was willing to face the risks of a strange country and to settle overseas.

This brings us to the second distinguishing characteristic of Greek life. The Greeks were by necessity a seafaring race, and so the economy of the Greek city-state could not long remain a self-sufficient agricultural economy; it was bound to develop on mercantile lines and to become dependent upon foreign trade. Whereas in the Eastern empires the traders were a small class in comparison with the great mass of peasants, in Greece trade permeated the whole of city life and its importance was vastly increased by colonial activity. Rival trade-leagues sprang up, and the first Greek war of which we have any record was probably between two such leagues competing for the western trade, the one headed by

Corinth, the other by Miletus. The date of the Lelantine war, as it was called, is about 700 B.C., and it left Corinth commercially supreme in the west, while Miletus maintained her power in the Black Sea.

Inevitably the growing influence of trade proved a no less disturbing factor in the domestic affairs of the city-states. The Greek city-state in 750 was usually ruled by an aristocracy or a king: the people met perhaps in a general assembly, but only to give its consent by acclaim to the dictates of its rulers. The aristocracy was an aristocracy of birth and land, and the trader belonged to the common people. Religion and justice alike were in the hands of those chosen families who by ancestral tradition claimed to know the ways of God and man. Such a political structure is suitable only to a stable agricultural community in which the wealth of the individual does not conflict with the interests of the people as a whole. But in the city-state agriculture was drawn into the orbit of trade as soon as the community ceased to be self-supporting. Whereas previously the merchant had imported only the luxuries of life and exported only the unwanted produce, now production began to be specifically for export, and cities became dependent upon imports for their raw materials. Corinth, for instance, began to monopolize the export of pottery to the west, and so became rapidly more and more dependent on imports for her food supply. The same thing happened in scores of towns.

The result was an ever deepening fissure between the supporters of the traditional and of the new way of life. The aristocracy was divided. Some sided with the new mercantilism, others fiercely opposed it; and a social struggle began between the old-fashioned landowners and the new traders. This struggle was intensified by the introduction of coinage about 650 B.C. For at first the control of the new means of exchange was not fully understood and for this reason it merely accentuated the social misery. The peasant proprietor was often bought up or enslaved: silver was hoarded and shortage of currency resulted in rising prices. Increasing misery brought political consciousness and the struggle between two rival groups of nobles became a social upheaval of the people claiming the right to live.

This social upheaval was the prelude to the second epoch of Greek history—the age of the Tyrants. Up and down the Greek world dictators supplanted the aristocrats and seized complete political control, supported frequently by the starving masses and by the merchants.

It is a queer accident that the word "tyrant," first used to describe these democratic dictators, should have come to mean a ruthless despot. Periander in Corinth, Peisistratus in Athens, and many others like them were men of great business ability and statesmanship who accommodated the political structure of their cities to the new economic conditions. They forged the bridge between aristocracy and constitutional government. Without their work Greece could not have developed that independence of spirit which was the source of her later brilliance and the chief cause of her success in the Persian wars.

The age of tyranny lasted from the middle of the seventh to the end of the sixth century. Throughout this century and a half one city after another succumbed to the economic crisis and the ensuing social revolution which passed from Asia Minor to mainland Greece and then spread all over the Greek world. It is impossible to overestimate the importance of this period in Greek history. Misunderstood by the later Greek philosophers and historians, neglected by some modern Hellenists who like to think of Greek culture as a unique spiritual phenomenon, remote from the petty considerations of money and trade, it was, in fact, the age in which were laid the foundations of the constitutional governments, legal codes, and philosophies of right which were the glory of classical Greece. It is as futile to disregard the age of tyranny in the study of Greek democracy as it would be to disregard the industrial revolution in an analysis of the modern Liberal State. As at the beginning of the last century industrialists and workmen united to sweep away an aristocratic regime, or to modify it to the new conditions, so in Greece the trader and the common people joined forces behind a tyrant to challenge the authority of the aristocracy of birth and land.

Thus it was the tyrants who really created the Greek *State*. They broke down the old tribal organization of primitive aristocracy and substituted for it a new patriotism: they destroyed local religious cults and replaced them by State-religions. By encouraging commerce they gained the loyalty of the merchant and manufacturer to the new regime: by stabilizing the currency and helping the peasant proprietor they restored agriculture to something like prosperity. Last, but not least, by breaking with the old tradition, they set free the spirit of reason and harnessed it to useful commercial ends. Tyranny was the government of the hard-headed business man who puts prosperity first in his political programme. As such it was a necessary stage in Greek development.

Of this new type of statesman, Peisistratus of Athens was perhaps the best example. In the colonizing period Athens had played no prominent part, but had solved her land problem by unifying Attica as a single State. Till the end of the seventh century she remained a small agricultural State, crippled in the closing years in her trade connections by the island power Aegina, just across the bay. But Athens could not avoid the economic crisis. After 630 social unrest increased steadily until supreme power was granted to *Solon* (one of the seven wise men of Greece). Solon tried to grapple with the problem by currency operations, cancellation of agricultural debt, and constitutional reform. But the conflict was too violent to be settled by peaceful means and the reforms he carried through in 594 B.C. were largely ineffective. Class-war grew yearly more violent, until Peisistratus in 560 B.C. seized control. Under his dictatorship Athens became a rich commercial state. The discovery of silver at Mount Laurium enabled her to mint a coinage famous throughout the Aegean: the concentration in agriculture upon the cultivation of the vine and olive made her a great exporting nation. She was able to provide the Black Sea towns with the wine and fats which they could not produce and in return to receive their flax and corn. Thirdly, she became the leading manufacturer of pottery and, with the friendship of Corinth, shipped her vases to cities all over the Mediterranean. Wealth brought culture: the tyrant's court was filled with poets; Athenian tragedy began and the Acropolis was adorned with those temples and statues whose fragments are now perhaps more highly prized than even the later products of the Periclean Age.

Throughout this period of colonial expansion and social revolution, one state in Greece had developed upon highly peculiar lines. Sparta, in the eighth century, was a normal Greek aristocracy, but it had solved its population problems not by sending out colonists, but by adding to its own Laconian territory the rich plain of Messenia. The Messenians became the serfs of the Spartan overlords, no better than the Helots in Laconia itself, and the new Sparta became a feudal State. About 650 the Messenians rose in revolt against the Spartans and for many years Sparta was torn by class-war. The Spartans were victorious; but they perceived that, if they were to secure themselves against future revolution, they could not afford the easy regime of earlier days. They must become a homogeneous and compact army, always on the watch for signs of social unrest. Within the citizen body there must be no inequalities of wealth or status such as would tempt the poorer classes to ally themselves with the serfs. But in the age of tyranny such inequalities were bound to arise through the new commercialism and the introduction of coinage. Towards the end of the seventh century, therefore, the Spartan constitution was radically reconstructed. The distinction of aristocrat and people was abolished and all Spartans were made equal; commerce was forbidden to any citizen on pain of expulsion, the land was redistributed, and coinage was banished for ever from Sparta. Sparta was fashioned into an equalitarian feudal State, in which power was divided between the two hereditary kings and the five ephors elected by the citizen Assembly.

But the reconstruction of the constitution was not enough. The serfs outnumbered the citizen body by fifteen to one, and revolution could only be suppressed by force of arms. Sparta therefore became an armed camp. A rigorous military education was introduced for boys and girls alike, luxury was forbidden to all, and a secret service was built up to keep watch upon the serfs. From now on the Spartans lived the life of foreign conquerors dominating and terrorizing a subject population, like the Spaniards in Mexico.

These changes insulated Sparta from the normal course of Greek development. While in the rest of Greece the influence of commerce broke up the old landed aristocracy, in Sparta feudalism was artificially preserved. Whereas elsewhere trade brought intercourse with foreign lands and stimulated the new culture and philosophy and science, in Sparta these were all sacrificed to the exigencies of the class-war. The Spartan army became the most powerful in all Greece, but it was used not to promote the interests of commerce abroad, but to preserve the feudal order at home.

For although at first the new regime showed imperial pretensions, and efforts were made to conquer the Peloponnese, it soon became clear that no Spartan army could venture far from home without the risk of a revolution occurring in its absence. Thus Sparta became the acknowledged leader of the Peloponnesian League, not by conquest, but by a series of loose alliances and mutual assistance pacts. Her neighbours acknowledged her hegemony with an easy mind, confident that she could not afford the luxuries of conquest and aggression.

Sparta was fated to be the greatest military power in all Greece, yet impotent to use this power effectively. Such a situation was bound to exasperate ambitious kings or generals; and when such men gained influence in Sparta, her foreign policy showed sudden vacillations. In each generation statesmen arose who tried to forge a Spartan Empire. At first they would be successful, but always they would end by arousing suspicion and fear in the minds of the citizens—and they would fall as suddenly as they had risen to power. Such men were Cleomenes at the end of the sixth century and his nephew Pausanias at the end of the Persian wars. In both cases a burning patriotism and imperial zeal were thwarted by the conservatism of a feudal State: in both cases great Spartan generals were forced to realize that only by emancipating the serfs could Sparta gain the inner vitality which empire demands. In both cases the suspicion that they harboured this design was largely responsible for their downfall.

From the middle of the sixth century Sparta and

Athens stood as prototypes of conflicting policies and contrasted philosophies. Athens represented the spirit of experiment, of commercialism, and of culture: Sparta was conservatism incarnate, resolutely opposed to tyranny and to democracy, and anxious to see in all the Greek cities the rule of the great landowner and the preservation of the aristocratic tradition.

In 546, at the height of Athenian prosperity, something happened far off in Asia Minor which was to change the whole course of European history. Sardis, capital of Lydia, was captured by Cyrus the Persian, and Greek independence was suddenly in danger of extinction. As we have seen, the Greek cities on the whole lived on friendly terms with their neighbours. In Asia Minor the kings of Lydia had from time to time made war upon them and subdued them, but their regime was not oppressive. Now in the course of thirty years a new empire arose to swallow up Babylon and Egypt, Phoenicia and Media and Lydia, and for the first time in history to organize an imperial government on a modern scale. Within a few years the Greeks of Asia Minor were a subject people, and by 510 it seemed clear that Persia would in time extend its control to mainland Greece.

It is important not to view this crisis through the eyes of succeeding generations. In 510 it must have seemed fantastic to suggest opposition to Persia. How could these hundreds of independent towns unite against a great imperial power? And, moreover, why should they do so? Greek commerce could continue as well under Persian rule, Greek wealth and prosperity would not be seriously affected by a centralized foreign empire. We must not imagine that any feeling of Greek solidarity was manifested at this time: on the contrary, Greek nationalism was the effect, not the cause, of the victories at Marathon and Salamis. The first serious result of the irruption of Persian power into Greek life was not unity but discord. Sparta was not deeply concerned by the news, and not even the warnings of King Cleomenes—then at the height of his power—could convince her that she had any responsibility or call to champion the cause of Greek independence. Sparta was concerned not for Greek independence but for the restoration of aristocratic government in the Greek towns, for the security of her position in the Peloponnese and for the maintenance of her military prestige. At Athens financial stringency was soon felt. For international trade was disturbed, the Egyptian market was closed, the Black Sea threatened, and the North Aegean silver mines lost. The tyranny which had given Athens peace and prosperity could not maintain its popularity through a period of depression, and in 510 Peisistratus' son, Hippias, was expelled.

But the expulsion of the tyrants solved no problem. Athens was leaderless and faction reappeared. Rival parties fought for power and "political associations" multiplied. It looked as though civil war was inevitable, and Sparta was only too willing to decide the issue in favour of the old aristocracy. At this moment, the Alcmaeonidae (a noble family of dubious commercial reputation) decided to make a bold bid for power. They had retained their trade connections

with the east throughout a long period of exile under
the tyranny: now they were concerned to strengthen
their newly won influence in the city. With this end
in view they introduced democracy and so gained
the solid support of the people for their commercial
interests (509–8). Their popularity was secured by
the ignominious expulsion from the city of Cleomenes,
who had appeared with a Spartan army to enforce
the restoration of the old aristocracy.

The democratic constitution set the seal on the work
of the tyranny, for it ensured the exclusion of the
large landowner from a predominating influence on
politics, and it put effective power into the hands of
the townsman—the merchant, the manufacturer, and
the proletariat.[1] And here we must note in passing
another distinctive feature of Greek life. The difference between aristocracy, oligarchy, and democracy
in Greece lay not in any principles, but in the dis-
position of privilege. Aristocracy meant a state where
the interests of the large landowner, oligarchy where

[1] The Athenian *proletariat* was composed of the free citizen
artisans and labourers, and must be distinguished both from the
slaves and from the resident foreigners. Living in the city and its
port at the Peiraeus, it could outvote the peasants in the Assembly,
and by manning the juries could dominate the law-courts. Its
interests during the epoch of expansion were closely allied with
those of the merchants, and since the oarsmen of the fleet were
drawn from its ranks, it could demand a considerable price for
its allegiance.

Thus while democracy in Greece was naturally connected with
naval power, aristocracy and oligarchy maintained the military
tradition. For a Greek army was recruited from the farmers and
the middle classes who could afford to buy their own arms and
equipment, while the navy depended on the town labourers.

those of the merchant and manufacturer, democracy where those of the town proletariat, predominated. Thus democracy was not the reconciliation of class-conflict but the pre-eminence of a single class.

The Alcmaeonidae hoped to remain masters in Athens owing to their popularity and the prosperity which trade would bring. But the international situation proved too difficult for them. Favouring as they did the interests of commerce, they wished to submit to Persia and to concentrate their military activities against Athens' trade rival—Aegina. But in Athens democracy had brought with it a wave of pan-Hellenic feeling which revolted against a tame submission, and when in 499 a revolt of the Greeks in Ionia broke out, Athens sent a small force to assist it and disowned the foreign policy of the Alcmaeonidae. The revolt was crushed, but henceforward Athens had to reckon with Persian hostility, and the young democracy found itself faced not only by a ring of Greek enemies, but by Persia as well.

At this moment a new statesman, Themistocles, rose to power: unlike the founders of democracy, he saw that the era of peaceful trade was over. If Athens was to survive and grow rich, she must arm and fight for her riches. Themistocles was the embodiment of a new democratic imperialism opposed alike to the conservative aristocracy and to the *laissez-faire* merchants who supported the Alcmaeonidae. More than any other man save Pericles, he set his stamp on Athenian democracy.

In 490 a small Persian force was beaten off at Marathon by the Athenian army, and for the next

ten years a fierce battle was waged in Athens between
the various political factions. The issue was decided
in 482, when Themistocles persuaded his countrymen
to employ the profits of a new silver vein at Laurium
for the construction of a huge fleet. From then on
Athens was an imperial maritime power, and in 480
it was she who was chiefly responsible for repelling
the full force of the Persian attack at Salamis, although
Sparta remained the official leader of the Greeks.

Salamis was the glorious justification of the new
Athenian democracy.[1] The town proletariat had
manned the fleet and proved that a few thousand
free citizens could defeat not only the conscript barbarians of the Persian Empire, but also the Greek
fleets which the Persians had compelled to attack
their kinsmen. At once the Greek cities of the Aegean
threw off the Persian yoke and acclaimed Athens as
their natural leader. In mainland Greece, however,
there was a certain resentment: the Peloponnese remained for the most part loyal to the Spartan con-
federacy, which after a reluctant participation in the
Persian wars showed no further interest in Greek
independence; and Northern Greece, which had been
largely pro-Persian, felt no great enthusiasm for the
new leader.

The results of the victory over the Persians were
profoundly important in the growth of the Greek

[1] It is significant that Plato in true aristocratic vein tried to
make Marathon, the land victory, the decisive battle of the wars,
and to relegate Salamis to second place. He could not concede
to the Athenian proletariat the credit for saving Greece! (See
Laws 707.)

mind. Sparta was forced by her domestic problems to resign her claim to be the champion of Greece, while Athens, transformed from a mercantile to an imperial power, welcomed her new pan-Hellenic responsibility to protect Greek independence from Persian aggression. To this end she formed the Delian League, an association of free cities pledged to provide the armaments necessary to maintain their freedom, and to open the seas again to Greek trade.

It was not till after the first flush of victory had faded away that the real problems arose. An uneasy alliance of Greek cities had defeated Persia and freed their compatriots: the Delian League had been formed. But how would these scores of city-states organize their freedom? Would they collaborate or would they fall into war and dissension again?

Such questions are seldom solved by discussion or by a rational and deliberate plan. We do not know of any suggestions at this time that the League should be turned into a real pan-Hellenic federation, and it is unlikely that they were made. For independence seemed essentially bound up with the structure of the city-state, and the sacrifice by any city of its sovereign rights would have been regarded as the sacrifice of freedom. For this reason the League was confined to the maritime cities of the Aegean, and the rest of the Greek world soon returned to its old inter-city rivalries. In Greece proper, for instance, Athens, Sparta, Corinth, Thebes, and Argos remained the dominant and rival powers.

In the Aegean the situation was different. Here, whatever the constitution of the Delian League, the

Athenian fleet was supreme: and gradually, partly
by accident, partly by design, the patron of freedom
became the tyrant whose power was used, not only
against Persia, but against recalcitrant members of the
League. By 450 the League was rapidly developing into
an Athenian Empire. The cities were still nominally
free, but the real sovereignty was in Athens. To
ensure the co-operation of her allies she imposed
democratic institutions, closely modelled on her own,
upon most of the cities: and, if resistance was offered,
governors and garrisons were sent out to preserve
order. The contributions for the upkeep of the anti-
Persian fleet became, in effect, taxes imposed by an
imperial power, and used by that power for its own
purposes; and a uniform Athenian coinage, which
most of the cities were forced to adopt, confirmed the
supremacy of Athenian trade. Even justice became
Athenian, since all capital offences and other important cases from the allied cities had to be tried at
Athens before an Athenian jury. And lastly, the
empire was strengthened at many strategic points by
Athenian colonies in the modern sense of the word—
organized settlements of Athenian citizens permitted
to occupy the land of their nominal allies.

But it must be repeated that Athens differed profoundly from a modern imperial power. Its situation
approximated far more to that of one member of the
League of Nations which managed to gain control of
the League machinery and use it for its own ends.
Theoretically in such a case the League would still be
a League, and the members independent nation-states.
Athens stood in some such relation to the Aegean

cities, and for this reason the transformation of the Delian League was not reflected in the speeches of the politicians until long after it had happened. Pericles, the greatest leader of the Athenian democracy, was, of course, fully aware of the course events were taking, but he still spoke the language of freedom to the assembled people, and stressed the responsibilities of Athens to the Greek world, not her power over it.

The history of the years 480 to 404 is little else than the story of the Athenian struggle to maintain and increase her maritime empire while entering on a fresh effort to conquer mainland Greece as well. For seventeen years conservative policy prevailed and Athens was fully employed in settling accounts with the Persians and in organizing the League, but at last, in 462, she felt strong enough to challenge Sparta and her confederates on land. Allying herself with Argos and with Thessaly, Athens essayed the conquest of mainland Greece. In the course of three short years Aegina—"the eyesore of the Peiraeus"—was suppressed, Greece as far south as the isthmus of Corinth was brought under Athenian control, and Corinthian trade in the west was threatened by Athenian pressure in the Gulf of Corinth.

Those years mark the zenith of Athenian democracy. The conservative policy of the aristocratic party had been content to share the hegemony of Greece with Sparta. Athens at sea and Sparta on land should work together in the service of Hellenic independence. This twofold leadership could only last so long as Athens did not threaten the commercial interests of

Sparta's confederates. For even if feudal Sparta had
no foreign aspirations, Corinth, her strongest ally, was
vitally concerned with the western trade routes, and
realized that as soon as the Aegean and the Levant
were secure, Athens would turn her attention to the
west. It was an Alcmaeonid—Pericles—who once
again broke the conservatives, denounced the Spartan
alliance, and proclaimed Athens' intentions to conquer
mainland Greece. He believed that compromise was
impossible—democracy must go forward or perish—
and so in domestic and foreign affairs he urged a
policy of ceaseless activity.

We still possess the war memorial on which are
inscribed the names of Athenians "who fell in the
same year in Cyprus, Egypt, and Phoenicia, at Halieis,
in Aegina and in Megara." Under the inspiration of
Pericles, Athens at the same time challenged the forces
of mainland Greece and launched an unprovoked
attack upon the Persians in Egypt, the granary of the
Levant. The democrats knew that their time was
short—they struck when the iron was hot. Almost
simultaneously, in Athens itself, the second stage of
the democratic revolution was pushed through. In
461 the Areopagus (the Athenian House of Lords)
was shorn of its power and the leading aristocratic
general was banished. The last defences of conservatism were broken through and supreme power
was granted to the people and to the people's chosen
leaders.

But Athens had overreached herself. In 454 came
the news that the Egyptian expedition had ended in
disaster. In Greece too Sparta had been roused from

her inertia and in 447 compelled Athens to surrender most of her land empire. At last, in 445, Pericles negotiated a thirty-years' peace with Sparta, and called a halt to allow democracy to recuperate before the next advance. But already the empire showed ominous signs of unrest. The second democratic revolution had given to the town proletariat well-nigh dictatorial power over the Assembly, the law-courts, and imperial policy. Although in 448 peace had been concluded with Persia, the new Athens could not afford to relax her imperial discipline, and the decisions of the Athenian law-courts—to which the League cities were forced to bring their cases—grew more and more flagrantly one-sided. Finally, the expenditure of vast sums on the Parthenon and other public buildings might seem to Pericles and to his friends a justifiable use of League moneys: to the allies it appeared to be the open proclamation of Athens' imperial designs. In 441 Samos, the wealthiest of the Greek islands, revolted and was only subdued after two years of siege.

In 432 came the beginning of the end. Though she had relinquished her empire, Athens still had designs on the western trade routes to Sicily and South Italy;[1] but in this field Corinth could brook no rival. Upon the pretext of a colonial dispute, war was declared and Corinth instigated a reluctant Sparta to put aside her domestic anxieties and face the menace of Athenian imperialism. The Greek world was divided into two factions and from 432 to 404 the Athenian navy was pitted against the armies of the Peloponnese.

[1] For a brief account of the Sicilian Greeks see page 248.

The final defeat of Athens was due to many causes. In the first place, the death of Pericles in the great plague which decimated the city left her leaderless, and the struggle of aristocrat against democrat and of town against country was disclosed in its full bitterness once his unifying personality was removed from politics. In the second place the deadlock produced by the conflict between an invincible army and an invincible navy was more bearable to the Spartans than to the impatient spirit of Athens. In the third place the war brought for Athens a financial stringency which was not felt in feudal Sparta, and increasing taxation made the allies yearly more restive. And in the fourth place, Athens in 413 lost the flower of her navy in a reckless attempt to conquer Sicily. From 411 to 404 Athens was convulsed by a series of revolutions culminating in an aristocratic *putsch* whose leaders eagerly made peace with Sparta and signed away the Athenian Empire. It was Sparta's turn to show if feudal aristocracy could rule with greater moderation and with stricter regard for justice than the democrats of Athens.

Such in barest outline is the story of the Athenian democracy and the Athenian Empire. Both began as institutions for the preservation and enlargement of freedom: both ended in tyrannical discord. They flourished only so long as there were statesmen in Athens able to dominate the popular assembly and to control its passions: and it is noteworthy that the rise of real proletarian leadership during the war against Sparta coincided with their decline. As soon as the people lost confidence in the statesmanship and *expertise* of the aristocracy, Athenian policy floundered into class-war and jingo imperialism; and from 425 on the empire and the democracy alike degenerated with astonishing rapidity, so that Plato, who was born in the year after Pericles died, held class-war and ruthless imperialism to be the inevitable accompaniments of popular self-government. From his own experience, he could come to no other conclusion.

But even in Periclean Athens, the evils were already latent. The so-called democracies of the allied towns were really the instruments of Athenian policy, and in Athens itself the struggle of rich against poor was beginning to destroy the basis of civic unity, already undermined by the growth of slavery (see Chapter 8). When we look at the Parthenon and read the funeral speech of Pericles we must not forget that the ideals which they express were only partially realized; and this partial realization was of brief duration. Ten years after Pericles' death, Athenian democracy meant not equality and liberty for all but the exclusion of the countryman and the aristocrat from the councils of the nation, and the confirmation of privilege to one class in the State. The Athenian Empire *did* for a time protect Greece from Persian aggression, but it also exposed scores of Greek cities to Athenian exploitation. On the other hand, to admit these defects is not to minimize the astonishing achievements of democratic Athens. Pericles was not exaggerating when he said:

"To sum up: I say that Athens is the school of Hellas, and that the individual Athenian in his own person seems to have the power of adapting himself to the most varied forms of action with the utmost versatility and grace. This is no passing and idle word, but truth and fact; and the assertion is verified by the position to which these qualities have raised the State. For in the hour of trial Athens alone among her contemporaries is superior to the report of her. No enemy who comes against her is indignant at the reverses which he sustains at the hands of such a city; no subject complains that his masters are unworthy of him. . . .

"I would have you day by day fix your eyes upon the greatness of Athens, until you become filled with the love of her; and when you are impressed by the spectacle of her glory, reflect that this empire has been acquired by men who knew their duty and had the courage to do it, who in the hour of conflict had the fear of dishonour always present to them, and who, if ever they failed in an enterprise, would not allow their virtues to be lost to their country, but freely gave their lives to her as the fairest offering which they could present at her feast. The sacrifice which they collectively made was individually repaid to them; for they received again each one for himself a praise which grows not old, and the noblest of all sepulchres—I speak not of that in which their remains are laid, but of that in which their glory survives, and is proclaimed always and on every fitting occasion both in word and deed. For the whole earth is the sepulchre of famous men; not only are they commemorated by columns and inscriptions in their own country, but in foreign lands there dwells also an unwritten memorial of them, graven not on stone but in the hearts of men. Make them your examples, esteeming courage to be freedom and freedom to be happiness. . . ."[1]

We must not forget these words when we examine Plato's condemnation of Athenian democracy. In it beauty was bound up with beastliness, rapacity with nobility, slavery with freedom. Athenian civilization, like every other civilization, contained within itself the seeds of its own destruction. Its flowers grew out of the dung of social conflict, but while they lasted they were of unmatched brilliance.

[1] *Thucydides*, II, 41, B. Jowett's translation.

3 SOCRATES

i. THE LIFE OF SOCRATES

IN the previous chapter we traced the history of the rise and fall of Athenian democracy. We must now turn our attention to the one Athenian of this period of whose personality we can claim to have intimate knowledge. If we look at the portraits which are preserved to us of the great politicians and poets of the fifth century—Aeschylus, Cimon, Themistocles, Alcibiades—we can admire their dignity and poise, but we cannot claim that they give us any understanding of the men whom they portray. They are types like the characters in Ben Jonson, not Shakespearian people. But even a second-rate copy of an original of Socrates is bursting with vitality. Not even the reticence and austerity of classical sculpture can prevent his personality from dominating the marble and breaking the sculptor's rules. We get the impression of an individual so unique and so vital that he cannot be fitted into any of the established types.

Who was this individual whose personality has endured when all the famous men of the period have become thin and ghostly shades, mere names appended to great events? Socrates was not a famous politician, but an ordinary Athenian citizen who served his city in the normal routine of peace and war. He was not a great artist or poet: though he wrote poems, they are not preserved. He was not even a scientist or philosopher, in the usual sense; for he made no discoveries, and, if he wrote any philosophy, not a word of his writings survive.

Socrates was not famous for anything—except for being Socrates. In a sense he did nothing, and yet he was and is one of the greatest figures of European civilization. Of him and of a few others—Jesus and St. Francis for instance—it can be truly said that their lives and individualities have moulded the shape of our innermost being and are still the inspiration of the best that is in us.

For this reason it is impossible to write an account of Socrates' teaching or to analyse and evaluate his philosophy. To understand Socratic philosophy it is necessary to know the man, and this can only be done by reading the Dialogues of Plato. For Plato devoted nearly all his literary activity to the composition of dialogues in which Socrates is the leading character. Many of them are highly realistic descriptions of actual conversations which took place before Plato was born: and to make them true to life Plato took enormous pains to reconstruct Periclean Athens and to recapture the spirit of Athenian democracy, which he himself had never known.

The chief justification for any description of Socrates is that it may persuade the reader to go to Plato himself and to read the *Apology*, the *Crito*, the *Phaedo*, the *Protagoras*, and the other dialogues in which Socrates' spirit has been so miraculously preserved. No modern account of Socrates can pretend to provide any real substitute for reading the dialogues themselves: and in this chapter there can

D

only be a bare outline of his life, and a bare
indication of the significance of his teaching.

Socrates was born in 469 B.C., ten years after the
battle of Salamis, and died in 399, four years after
Athens had capitulated to Sparta. Thus he lived
through the period of Athens' greatest glory and
greatest humiliation. Scarcely a year of his life passed
without some notable victory or defeat for his native
country. He was an Athenian citizen of respectable
family and, like all citizens of Athens, he spent a
considerable amount of time on active service, and
on two occasions at least we hear of his courage on
the field of battle. But the first forty years of his
life were otherwise uneventful. As far as we know,
he took no part in politics until he was an old man,[1]
and throughout the stress and clamour of the years
in which Athens was struggling to achieve supremacy
on sea and land, he did no more than fulfil the
routine obligations of citizenship and enjoy the life
of Periclean Athens.

Socrates was above all things a citizen of Athens.
He loved the city, with its glorious buildings and its
thriving port—the metropolis of the Aegean. He was
proud to claim the privileges of Athenian citizenship
and to feel that he was a living part of the city which
was "the school of Hellas." Unhindered by aristocratic snobbery or political prejudices, he mixed with
all sorts and conditions of men, and in democratic
Athens he could talk to generals and statesmen, to
artists and craftsmen, to philosophers and scientists,
with the easy openness and equality of which Pericles

[1] See page 141.

spoke in his funeral speech. For Athens in the days of her greatness attracted to her everything that was good in Hellenic culture, and within her walls a man could learn to know at first hand all the "glories that were Greece."

It is therefore not surprising that Socrates for most of his life was content to live quietly in Athens. At first he was probably best known for his extraordinary appearance. A small, scrubby man, thick-set and clumsy, with an enormous head, and eyes sunk deep below a bulging forehead—he was likened by his contemporaries to an ugly satyr. But if his appearance was ludicrous he was feared by everyone with whom he talked for his sardonic humour and his "Socratic irony," that naïve innocence and apparent ignorance which could with a single simple question explode a pretentious theory and "debunk" hypocrisy. The few who knew him really well loved him for the friendliness which lurked under his grim exterior and the honesty which made his debunking not mere cleverness but a genuine effort to sift truth from falsehood.

About 430 Socrates suddenly became a public figure. The Oracle at Delphi was still respected by all Greece as the voice of Apollo. Before any important enterprise every city would send an embassy to discover whether Apollo was favourable and, for a fee, the Delphic priests would conduct the prophetess to the Holy Chasm, where, inspired with mysterious fumes, she "spoke with tongues," and her words were interpreted by the priests into riddling poems. The embassy would then return home and seek to elucidate the meaning of the Oracle. That the Oracle was corruptible had been proved on many occasions. The Alcmaeonidae had found it useful and had paid for its services by rebuilding the temple. It had been notoriously pro-Persian in 480, and in return the Persian invaders had left its riches untouched. And yet Delphi was still respected. For its priests were always well-informed and a "tip" from the Oracle had often saved a city or an individual from destruction. It was therefore no small thing when in answer to a question from one of Socrates' devotees, the Oracle declared him the wisest man in all Greece.

It is difficult to analyse Socrates' feelings when he heard the news. For all his rationalism, he was, as we shall see later, a religious man; and though he may have doubted the motives of the priests, he must have felt that in some sense God had spoken and declared that he knew what no other man knew. This fact gave him a new sense of vocation. Hitherto he had been content to enjoy the pleasures of Athenian society: now he became urgently aware of a duty which he must perform and a mission he must fulfil. No sudden change of life was demanded of him—to the outside observer he behaved precisely as he had behaved before—but the life he had led became charged with a new significance as he perceived that what he had previously done through natural curiosity and dislike of humbug was something essential to the salvation of the Athens which he loved.

To understand the mission to which Socrates from

now on devoted his life and in the fulfilment of which he was finally to die, we must consider the effect of the political and social upheavals of the previous hundred years upon the life of the individual Athenian. The democratic revolution had shaken morality and religion to their very foundations. Not only in Athens, but all over the Greek world, the destruction of aristocratic authority had brought with it a freedom of spirit new in the history of mankind, a distrust of authority not only in the political but in the religious sphere, and a reliance on human reason as the only proper instrument for the solution of every problem.

To appreciate this intellectual revolution we have only to consider the effects of the industrial revolution upon the morality and religion of our own age. Here, too, a new class of manufacturers and technicians pushed its way into political power: an old technique of production and distribution was replaced by a new one, and the class-structure of society was radically reshaped. These political and social changes were accompanied by an intellectual revolution no less profound than they. The established order of scientific and ethical philosophy and the established institutions of religion were not adapted to the needs of the new industrial society. As liberalism challenged the political *status quo*, so Darwinism challenged the dogmas of the Churches. In the triumph of liberalism, it was not only the statesmen and the manufacturer who were responsible for victory: the scientist and the philosopher also played their part.

The developments in Greece were precisely parallel, save that here the revolutionary process was unprecedented in world history. If we think for a moment of the great civilizations of Babylon, Egypt and Crete which preceded that of the Greeks, we shall see that religion and reason were there kept rigidly apart. Reason or intelligence was regarded as useful in ordinary life—the craftsman, the sailor, and the general all applied it to the problems which faced them—but there was a whole sphere of life where the ordinary man was forbidden to use his intelligence at all. He must not dispute how the world came to be, how the gods ruled the world, what was right and wrong, how sin could be expiated. These questions were holy and they could be answered only by holy men. Only the priest had access to the gods. To the ordinary mortal it was forbidden. He must be content to accept the answers which the priests gave him, and he must accept them, not because he saw that they were true, but because the authority of the priest was absolute. The Greeks tore down this dividing wall between religion and intelligence. They challenged the authority of the priest and set up reason or intelligence as the sole arbiter of what is acceptable and what is not. In one sense nothing was holy to them because nothing was left unchallenged by reason; in another sense everything was holy because they believed everything was intelligible, finite, clear-cut and amenable to the law of Reason. It is often said that the Greeks were irreligious people. To say that is to make religion nothing better than superstition. True religion cannot forbid the use of reason, or deny the possibility of truth. It was a deeply religious feeling which inspired the Greek belief that we can understand the world around us, and break down the tabus which lurk in every mountain and tree and stream; and it was a profound sense of morality which questioned the primitive religion of human sacrifice and denied the existence of jealous and licentious gods. The early Greek philosophers were not free-thinkers or material-ists, but pious and devout men who discovered that reason can free mankind from fear and hatred, and teach him the nature of reality. Their speculations were at the same time an analysis of natural and of religious phenomena: and thus they were both the first scientists and the first theologians.

For this reason we find in the fragments of their writings which we possess a moral exaltation matched by few passages in the Hebrew prophets. In the Old Testament we are still for the most part in a world of jealousy and fear. God is still the possession of a people or tribe. Ritual and ceremonial are con-fused with morality, and symbols take the place of intellectual concepts. Sublime visions are dimly seen, but they remain visions, unclarified by reason or analysis. To turn from the Hebrew prophets to the Greek thinkers of the sixth century is to move into another world, remote from our own, and yet far more akin to it. For here are men, conscious of the reason which distinguishes them from beasts, and resolved to break through the curtains of symbol and ritual and ceremony, and to see the reality behind them face to face. The enterprise is dangerous, but it must be attempted. If man is to follow his divine calling and become rational, then first of all religion and morality must become rational too.

How closely this attack on priestly authority was connected with the social revolution is shown by the fact that it began in Asia Minor and South Italy in the middle of the age of tyranny. One after another thinkers arose to substitute for the myths and cosmogonies, which had previously been taken on trust, new scientific accounts of the way that the world came to be. These early philosophies seem crude and laughable to-day: Thales, for instance, declared everything to be water. But such a theory was in reality an amazing advance of human reason. Thales had observed that ice, which is solid, turns into water, water into steam; and he had further noticed how the steam or mist often seems to be drawn up by the sun. He concluded that there were four prime substances, earth, air, fire, and water, which were transformed into one another in a regular cyclical process. What is important is not the theory but the method. He was trying to give an account of the world which squared with his observations, and he was searching for substances whose changes could be understood and shown to account for the observed changes in nature. We have only to contrast Thales' philosophy with the first chapter of the book of Genesis or the Greek myths to appreciate his achievement. From this date (about 580) no religion or theology or myth could satisfy the Greek thinker which had not been tested by reason and comparison.

Fifty years later in South Italy the second discovery

was made. Pythagoras, half mystic and half scientist, the vegetarian believer in the transmigration of souls, founded the study of Pure Mathematics, and may actually have discovered the theorem which bears his name. Imbued with a profound veneration for magic numbers and figures, he found that these holy entities had properties of their own which only pure thought could discern; a worshipper of the heavenly bodies, he maintained that they moved not in a mysterious but in a mathematical way; trained to find in musical incantations the way to religious ecstasy, he discovered that behind the audible melody there lay numerical ratios, not heard but understood. In the course of the next half century his followers had laid the foundations of astronomy, geometry, and harmonics. These sciences seemed to their earliest devotees in no way contradictory to religion, but the beginnings of a new theology which must finally disclose the nature of the supreme perfect Cause whom no eyes could see, the Eternal Being, rational and immutable, the Pure Intelligible Godhead.

But although the early Greek philosophers were theologians "intoxicated with reason," to whom it was self-evident that truth was the only priestess and reason the only oracle of true religion, the effect of their teaching on Greek society was revolutionary. Freed from all authority and restraint, Greek thought roamed at large over the universe, questioning and denying the accepted order of things. The collapse of religious authority confirmed the political and social collapse of the aristocratic tradition. The first results were therefore not a new intellectual discipline to replace the old traditions, but intellectual and social rebellion. Man, it was felt, had at last been freed from bondage to superstition and from subjection to absolutism. Since reason and intelligence were now the standards by which worth was measured, the aristocrat and the priest could be treated as ordinary men and judged on their merits. In future no one's opinion should carry extra weight because of his family tree or social position or holy office.

Thus the cult of reason developed into an individualist and equalitarian philosophy, which threatened to break up the whole fabric of society. Where each man is as good as his neighbour, political parties are inevitable; and the Greek city became a whirlpool of political intrigue. Where there are political parties there must be propaganda; and rhetoric and oratory became essential to the citizen of a democracy who wanted to compete for social or economic or political success. Where rhetoric is supreme, the decision of the law-courts will be swayed by brilliant argument and appeals to the emotions; and so in the law-courts it was persuasion, not truth, which prevailed. A policy, a point of view, a moral principle or a religion came to be valued not for its truth, but for its popular appeal, just as the goodness of an article in modern life is sometimes assessed by its sales. In the end the substitution of reason for tradition as the supreme criterion produced not freedom for the individual, as had been hoped, but power for the few individuals who were skilled in the arts of salesmanship.

Another result of these changes was the vogue for science and philosophy amongst the leisured classes.

Knowledge and education became fashionable, and the demand for scientific lectures was satisfied by the Sophists, experts who travelled from town to town, living on their lecture fees. They gave courses in medicine, astronomy, mathematics, civics, theology, and anything else for which there was a demand. The demand was forthcoming; for education had become both a fashion and a necessity in the new commercial society.

Of all the courses which they provided, the most popular and the most dangerous was rhetoric, the art of propaganda. In democratic Athens, with its passion for litigation, rhetoric seemed essential to any happiness. It brought political power, wealth, and personal success. For rhetoric—like propaganda and advertising—was the art of making others agree to a point of view whether that point of view was right or wrong. Indeed, the falser it was the greater the rhetorical success in persuading someone else to accept it: and conversely, the sounder a doctrine or a legal case or a political judgment, the more the skill required to make it look ridiculous. Rhetoric, in fact, was the technique of making the worse appear the better and the better the worse cause. Its connection with the Sophists is shown by our modern word *sophistical*, and it rapidly became the most highly developed science in all Greece.

Such was the atmosphere in which Socrates grew up. As a young man he plunged enthusiastically into the maelstrom of new ideas, reading and listening to the famous lecturers, even arguing with Zeno and

Parmenides, the propounders of the latest paradoxes of western Greek philosophy. But soon he began to feel lost in the buzz of speculation and dialectical cleverness.

A whole-hearted rationalist, he accepted the revolt of reason and its refusal to be bound by prejudice and by tradition. Greedy for the new science and philosophy, he participated eagerly in the Athenian renaissance and welcomed the new education which the Sophists offered. Endowed with an overwhelming sense of the value of personality and of true self-realization, he could not deny that the challenge to the established order had left the individual free to develop his own talents and his own apprehension of truth and that the Sophists provided the means to this self-development. But when he examined Athenian society, he began to see that the old superstitions had been replaced by a materialistic philosophy, and the old education by lessons in salesmanship and propaganda. Just as democracy by 430 meant not freedom for all, but privilege and political power for one class, so rationalism was coming to mean, not the destruction of all prejudice, but the replacement of one type by another. Education was not valued as an end in itself, but purchased as a useful weapon for the social struggle.

Up till the moment when the Oracle was given, Socrates had been an amused and somewhat cynical spectator of the Athenian renaissance. He had enjoyed picking holes in pretentious theories and exposing the illogicalities in the arguments of the philosophers, and he had not resisted the temptation to apply his destructive criticism to distinguished statesmen and poets. But he had done this with a light heart. Now he admitted to himself what he had long suspected. Life in Athens might well be a glorious adventure, but it was high time to ask precisely where Athens stood, what the democratic revolution really meant, what the empire really was, and what freedom of thought really implied. The last hundred years had been a period of such colossal changes that no one had had time to stop and consider their significance. The social process had swept Athens along so fast that no Athenian had had time to see where Athens was going. Each stage had seemed inevitable, and the pace had been so rapid that there had only been time to prepare for the next stage without asking too carefully about the direction or the final goal. Now, in Socrates' view, it was time to call a halt and ask those quite simple questions to which everyone had a ready answer on his lips, but about which few had seriously pondered.

This, then, was his vocation, and this was the meaning of Apollo's words. Socrates, the man who claimed that he knew nothing, was the wisest man in Greece precisely because he alone realized that the fundamental questions were not being asked by the Sophists and the statesmen and the 'educated' Athenians. They thought they knew the answers, when they did not. He at least recognized his own ignorance. Let us hear his own description of the matter:

"When I heard the answer of the Oracle, I said to myself: 'What on earth can the god mean by this riddle? I am not conscious of having any wisdom either small or great. What can he mean by calling me the wisest of men? He cannot be telling a lie; for that would be against the law of his nature.' For a long time I pondered what he could mean, and then very reluctantly I decided to put the Oracle to the proof. So I went to a man with a great reputation for wisdom, in the hope that I could thereby refute the Oracle and say to the god, 'You said I was the wisest of men, but here is someone who is wiser than I.' The gentleman I approached was a politician—I need not mention his name—and I examined him very carefully. But the result was that after conversation with him I realized that, although in his own estimation and in that of many others he was a wise man, in fact he was nothing of the kind. So then I tried to show him that he thought himself wise but was not really wise, and the consequence was that I made an enemy of him and many of those present. So I left him saying to myself, 'I really am wiser than this gentleman. I suppose neither of us knows anything beautiful and good: but whereas he thinks he knows something when he doesn't, I do at least realize my own ignorance. In this single trifling way I suppose I am wiser than he.' Then I went to someone else with a reputation even greater than his, but I came to the selfsame conclusion about him. And so I made an enemy of him too and of many others besides."[1]

In this passage Socrates indicated what he held to be the fundamental weakness of Athenian society. The democratic revolution had swept away the old

[1] See *Apology*, chapter 21.

established order. The authority of priest and noble had been replaced by the autonomy of individual reason. But reason must not only destroy the temple of superstition: it must erect a new temple to replace it, more ordered, more beautiful and more true than the old. To awaken Athens to this task was the bounden duty of any patriot.

Socrates devoted the last twenty years of his life to the fulfilment of this duty—the exposure of ignorance in high places. The ordinary Athenian saw in him only a typical Sophist, as he sat, day by day, surrounded by clever young men, demolishing the pretensions of highly respectable citizens. But, unlike the Sophists, Socrates charged no fees. Disclaiming all knowledge, he declared himself incompetent to teach, and claimed that he was merely trying to discover the truth. If anyone should pay, it was he, for he was always the pupil, never the master. This humility naturally infuriated anyone who had been subjected to the deadly Socratic analysis and had been forced to realize his state of mental confusion. For it soon became clear that no reputation could survive a conversation with Socrates, the man who knew nothing.

A few of his closest friends, among them Plato, had some inkling of the meaning of his life: but the conservative politician soon recognized him as a danger to Athenian democracy. In 423 the playwright Aristophanes attacked him bitterly as a scientific buffoon, a dangerous radical who ridiculed sound tradition and made decent men look fools. Aristophanes' criticism was largely justified: a degenerate aristocracy hung on Socrates' words and utilized his arguments to discredit the democracy which they wished to supplant. Alcibiades and Critias and their friends were only waiting their chance to overthrow the regime and inaugurate the counter-revolution: Socrates' methods supplied them with fresh ammunition, which they used unscrupulously against their democratic opponents. They learnt his dialectical methods and used them, not as Socrates used them to expose half-truth, but to annihilate truth.

We must remember that the last thirty years of Socrates' life were lived in a period of almost unbroken war. Athens was fighting for her existence, and it was clear that defeat would mean an aristocratic counter-revolution. For this reason the party conflict became ferociously bitter, and any criticism of democracy was taken to imply support for the aristocratic opposition. However scrupulously Socrates avoided taking sides, he could not pretend that democracy was perfect or veil his contempt for many of its spokesmen. Nor could he deny his association with Alcibiades and Critias, or avoid responsibility for their chequered careers. By his exposure of ignorance wherever he found it, he had weakened the Government and strengthened the opposition.

In 404 Critias and his friends at last made their *putsch*, set up the regime of the thirty tyrants, and capitulated to Sparta. Socrates took no part whatsoever in their conspiracy: and when an attempt was made to implicate him in its crimes, by instructing him to arrest a wealthy citizen, his refusal nearly cost him his life. But the fact that Critias was his pupil could not be gainsaid. When the democracy was restored he was arrested and put on his trial ostensibly for worshipping strange gods and corrupting the youth, actually for aiding and abetting the counter-revolution.

It is probable that the new democracy was reluctant to push the matter to a conclusion. The legal case against Socrates was known to be weak; his honesty and integrity were widely recognized, and the temper of the day was inclined to toleration. But Socrates was now seventy years old: the Athens he had loved was gone, never to be rebuilt. Almost deliberately he seemed to press for a final decision, refusing absolutely to escape from prison or to accept the various offers of help which came from his many friends. He felt that he had lived his life in the service of Athens. It was for her sake that he had exposed the ignorance of her politicians and the corruption of her social life. But his criticism had been either un-heeded or reviled or perverted, and now he felt sure that only his death could effect what his life had failed to achieve. If he were prepared to die at the order of the city which he had served, then perhaps his example would inspire others to continue the work which he had begun.

And so he remained in prison awaiting death and talking happily to his friends. Right to the end his loyalty never wavered. When Crito urged him once more to escape, he only replied: "Surely you must see that your country is something which you must honour and revere more even than your father or mother or forefathers. In the eyes of God and of men of understanding it has a higher claim on you than all of these. If it is angry with you, you must behave towards it with more deference and humility than you do even to your father; and you must either persuade it that you are right or else you must do as it commands and suffer as it commands without complaint. If it orders you to be beaten or imprisoned, if it sends you to war to be wounded or killed—still you must obey. For it has the right to demand this of you, and you must not flinch or draw back or desert your post. On the field of battle, in the courts of law and in all your daily life, you must do whatever the city, which is your country, commands; or else you must succeed in convincing it that you are in the right. To use force against your mother or your father is wicked. How much more so against your country!"[1]

At his trial, too, he deliberately courted death. Refusing to use the usual appeals *ad misericordiam*, he made his speech for the defence into a brilliant and humorous justification of his whole life. It was his patriotism, he urged, which made it impossible to retract what he had said, or to give an assurance for the future that he would soften his criticism. Finally, when, according to Athenian practice, he was asked to assess his penalty, he replied that the only penalty which he deserved was a free meal daily in the town hall as a reward for his services. He was condemned by a small majority to die by drinking hemlock.

The last hours of his life were spent in conversation with his friends. Plato has preserved for us an account

[1] *Crito*, chapter 12.

of them in his dialogue the *Phaedo*, and has painted the final scene.

"He took the cup quite serenely, without a tremor or any change of colour or expression, looking steadily at the warder with that peculiar stare of his. Then he said, 'What about pouring a libation? May I?' The warder answered, 'We only prepare just the correct amount.' 'I see,' said he, 'but I may and must pray to the gods that my journey from this world to the other may be blessed. That then is my prayer. So be it!' As he said this he raised the cup and drank it off quite cheerfully and calmly. Up till then most of us had been able to restrain our tears fairly well: but when we saw him drinking and when we saw that he had drunk the poison, we could do so no longer. In spite of myself, my tears poured down, and I put my cloak over my face and wept. It was not for him that I wept but for my own bereavement. Crito had been unable to restrain his tears and had got up before me and gone aside. Apollodorus too had been weeping all the time, and now he cried out loud and his passionate outburst made us all break down. Only Socrates remained calm and said, 'Come! Come! What are you doing! The chief reason why I sent the women away was to prevent this sort of scene; for I have been told that death should come to a man in a holy peace. Please be patient and calm.' At these words we felt ashamed and controlled our tears. Then he began to walk about until he said that his legs were feeling heavy, and lay down on his back, as the warder instructed him. The man who had given him the poison every now and then examined him, pressing his feet and his legs, and then he queezed his foot hard and asked if Socrates felt anything. Socrates said no. So he squeezed his shins and, moving gradually up the body, showed us that he was growing cold and stiff. Then he pressed hard again and said that when it reached his heart, he would be gone.

"Socrates had covered his face with his cloak, but when the chill reached his groin, he pushed back the cloak from his face and said (these were his last words), 'Crito, we owe a cock to Aesculapius: don't forget to pay the debt.' Crito said, 'Very well, Socrates. Is there anything else?' Socrates gave no answer to this question, but after a little while he stirred. The warder uncovered him and his eyes were glazed. Crito saw this and closed the eyelids and the mouth.

"So Socrates, our friend, died. Of all the men of his time whom any of us met, not one was as fine or as wise or as good as he."

ii. THE TEACHINGS OF SOCRATES

Socrates was condemned to death for corrupting the youth and for worshipping strange gods. From what we have seen of his life, this charge seems so fantastic that it can hardly have been seriously put forward. And yet we shall find that the jury's verdict was politically justifiable. Socrates, the patriotic Athenian and the devoted searcher after truth, was partially responsible for accelerating the Athenian collapse and still further disintegrating the social life of Athens.

His philosophy, because it was incomplete, was pernicious.

Had this not been the case Plato might never have written his *Republic*. For it was the fact that the noblest man whom he had known had been justifiably condemned to death which first forced him to realize the tragic dilemma of Greek civilization, and made him take upon himself the completion of the task which Socrates had left unfinished. To understand Plato we must try to see why Socrates was condemned to death. In so doing we shall perhaps perceive something of the nature of his philosophy.

We have seen that Socrates was deeply perturbed by the Athenian complacency at the destruction of the old aristocratic religion and morality. He saw that intellectual freedom degenerates into mere licence unless the free individual voluntarily subjects himself to a new rational discipline. The old aristocratic order had imposed a discipline and an education upon the citizen. It had trained him for war and given him a rigid standard of right and wrong. It had provided an education, though not a rational one. Inevitably, therefore, the age of reason must develop a rational system of education, if it was to bring happiness and not misery to men.

Socrates called the new education of which he dreamed *philosophy*—the search for wisdom. Athens must be taught not to accept traditional morality, but to discover rational principles of conduct and to base its social life upon them. The old education had consisted in putting into the minds of the young the orthodox ideas about right and wrong: the new philosophy would try to develop the individual reason in each man so that he only accepted those ideas which he saw to be true and rejected all wickedness, not from fear of punishment but because he understood its folly.

Thus philosophy, according to Socrates, must be the self-discipline of reason, and it had two main tasks: (1) to examine and to reject those opinions which it found to be false, and (2) to substitute for these false opinions a new set of principles acceptable to reason. The method of this new education was extremely simple: it consisted of asking for definitions of every-day words like "justice" or "courage" or "piety" and, by a process of discussion, sifting the false from the true. Socrates did not claim that in these discussions he taught anybody anything at all, but only that he helped others to discover what they really knew already. He did not provide his hearers with new and interesting ideas, but like a midwife assisted the pregnant mind to bring forth its own truths. In the early dialogues of Plato we can watch "the midwife" at work. He is usually in conversation with an expert or a prominent citizen and after a few minutes of desultory talk pounces on some word which his opponent has used. What, he asks in conversation with a general, does courage mean precisely? The general must clearly know in order to do his job properly. But the general cannot precisely define it and is caught in a maze of inconsistencies. Various definitions are tried, but even those suggested by Socrates are found to be deficient and the dialogue ends in a complete breakdown.

The only positive result seems to be that one more human being realizes that he does not know what he means by the very simplest words he uses and detests Socrates for having brought him to this realization.

On first reading, these dialogues seem entirely destructive. Frequently the argument is unsound and Socrates is guilty of what looks like deliberate unfairness. The modern reader will sympathize with the jury who condemned him, and ask what possible use his verbal cleverness can be. But if we study them more carefully we shall notice that—however negative the conclusions may be—these dialogues are in one sense positive. They are examples of an educational method. This method of *analysis*—the attempt to define precisely the meanings of common words—is the great contribution of Socrates to modern philosophy; for if we do not know precisely the meanings of the words we use, we cannot discuss anything profitably. Most of the futile arguments on which we all waste time are largely due to the fact that we each have our own vague meanings for the words we use and assume that our opponents are using them in the same senses. If we defined our terms to start with, we could have far more profitable discussions. Again, we have only to read the daily papers to observe that propaganda (the modern counterpart of rhetoric) depends largely for its success on confusing the meaning of the terms. If politicians were compelled by law to define any term they wished to use, they would lose most of their popular appeal, their speeches would be shorter, and many of their disagreements would be found to be purely verbal. Thus Socrates believed that the first task of philosophy was to clear away confusion and mis-representation by defining the meanings of words.

But that was only a preliminary. The true task of philosophy was not to define words but to discover reality. As we have seen, Socrates had studied the attempts of the scientists and the mathematicians to find in the workings of nature a rational plan. Mathematics had disclosed the possibility of deductive proof and logical certainty. No one who had once understood Pythagoras' theorem could doubt it or regard it as merely probable: for the mathematician it was eternally and absolutely true. Socrates observed that mathematics depended on precise definitions of terms, but he also noticed that it did not consist solely of definitions: it was an ordered and consistent body of knowledge. It seemed to him possible to apply to human relations the mathematical method, and he believed this to be the task of philosophy. If we could know justice and truth and beauty, understanding their properties and inter-relations as we understand Euclid, then life would be rational and happy. What the scientists and mathematicians were doing for the world of nature, philosophy must accomplish for human society.

The philosophical discipline is never popular: it is indeed the most exasperating torture to which the human mind can be subjected. It hunts out our dearest prejudices and shows that they have no rational foundations, and it exposes what we thought to be a logical theory as a mass of contradictions. Although it is directed to the development of the individual, it does not satisfy our ordinary ideas of self-realization since it calls on each of us to relegate most of his personal interests to second place. It does not press for the free development of individual tastes, but demands that the individual should voluntarily regulate his life by the dictates of reason.

Socrates believed that this discipline alone could save Athenian democracy from collapse. Now that the bonds of tradition had been broken, the individual citizen must forge for himself the new morality. And education must be concerned to produce that change of heart which was necessary if he was to be willing to undertake these great responsibilities. For this reason Socrates was as much opposed to the type of culture and education which the Sophists were popularizing, as he was to the point of view of the ordinary uneducated business man. He saw that education and intellectual training can be used for purely materialist ends. Men can be naturally clever and highly educated, and yet totally unphilosophic. They can allow reason to be the slave of their passions, or of other people's passions: and education can be merely a useful weapon in the class-struggle. Socrates believed that the teaching provided by the Sophists was little better than this. It gave to men techniques for getting what they wanted, and the Sophists were interested not in the spiritual health of their pupils but in providing something useful for which people were prepared to pay. Socrates agreed with the conservatives that such education was no substitute for the old-fashioned discipline of aristocratic Athens. It put new power into the hands of the intellectual, but it gave him no principles for the use of that power. For this reason it produced a reckless individualism and disregard for the good of the community. Once the restraints of morality and religion had been destroyed, the individual citizen was free to do as he pleased; and education was merely embittering the class-struggle instead of healing it.

This, in Socrates' view, was the disease from which Athenian democracy was suffering. Class-conflict and imperialism were the results of a *laissez-faire* philosophy of individual licence; and if Reason could not produce a new self-discipline, then the belief that right is might would rule in Athens. As the great war dragged on, it became yearly more clear that this was happening. For all its faults, Athens in the age of Pericles had been inspired by an exalted patriotism and a real sense of pan-Hellenic responsibility. Now these motives were being submerged by faction and self-interest. No impartial observer could deny the terrible decline in the standards of Athenian life which set in after the death of Pericles.

The most sober and therefore the most ruthless critic of this degeneration was Thucydides, an Athenian general exiled for his failure on a campaign, who composed a detailed history of the great war between Athens and Sparta. One quotation is sufficient to indicate the analysis which he made. It is taken from 'the Melian dialogue' in which Thucydides describes how Athens subdued a small island called Melos.[1]

[1] For a complete version see *Thucydides* V, 85, Everyman's Edition.

"Athens also made an expedition against Melos. The Melians are of Spartan descent and were therefore unwilling to become subject to Athens. At first they remained neutral. Then when Athens committed acts of wanton aggression, they were forced into open warfare. Athens sent an expeditionary force but before opening hostilities the Athenian generals entered into negotiations with the Melians. The following conversations ensued:

ATHENS: We do not intend to waste time making flowery speeches to justify our Empire on the ground of our services to Greece against Persia, or to pretend that our present invasion is motivated by any past misdemeanours of yours. We suggest, therefore, that you, too, should omit such arguments. Do not waste time describing how, although you are of Spartan descent, you have not joined the Spartan alliance against us, or how our aggression is unprovoked. Let us negotiate on the basis of our real feelings and of the situation as it really is. We all know that justice in this world is only possible between two powers of equal strength. Power extorts all it can: weakness concedes all it must. We are here to strengthen our Empire. We wish to include you within it with a minimum of trouble, in order that your existence in future may be of profit to us both.
MELOS: You will certainly benefit from conquering us. How should we benefit by accepting subjection to you?
ATHENS: You would have the advantage of submitting before the worst occurred: we should gain by not destroying one of our subjects.

MELOS: You refuse then to allow us to remain neutral and on friendly terms with you?

ATHENS: Yes, in the eyes of our subjects your neutrality is a sign of our weakness: your hostility will occasion a display of our strength. Our subjects believe that if any state maintains its independence the reason is to be found in its strength which makes us hesitate to attack it. Your subjection, therefore, would at the same time extend our Empire and increase our security.

MELOS: But surely your security would be best advanced if we remain neutral; for if you attack us, you will alienate the sympathies of all the states which are now neutral. When they see how you are treating us, they will expect their turn to come soon. In fact, you will be strengthening the forces against you and driving anyone who has not yet taken sides into the enemy camp. Furthermore, if you are willing to take the risks which you admit are necessary to maintain your Empire, you must agree that we should show a contemptible lack of spirit if we do not do everything we can to preserve the independence we still possess.

ATHENS: Not if you take an objective view of the matter. You have not to decide whether you should engage in a war between two forces equally matched, but how you can preserve yourselves against an enemy of vastly superior strength. The question is not one of honour but of prudence.

MELOS: But we know that victory does not always go to the big battalions. If we surrender now we give up *all* hope; if we fight, there is at least a chance we may survive.

ATHENS: Hope is indeed very comforting in moments of danger, and those who have something else to depend on may not be ruined by accepting her comforts. But do not be deluded by hopes. Though your position is desperate, a rational method of self-preservation is still open to you. Do not make the silly mistake of pinning your hopes in such a situation upon the supernatural and upon the favours of heaven.

MELOS: We recognize the danger we are in. But our cause is just and yours is not, and in the eyes of God we shall at least find no less favour than you. As for our weakness, it will be compensated by the support of the Spartans. They are of common stock with us and cannot refuse us help. Our confidence, therefore, is not so blind as you suppose.

ATHENS: We expect to receive quite as much favour from on high as you. Our attitude in religious matters is scrupulously correct: our mundane aims are not abnormal. There is a law of nature which declares that every living creature extends its empire to the limits of its power. We know this is true of the human species: we believe that it applies in heaven as well. We did not make this law, nor were we the first to implement it. We inherited it from our fathers, we act upon it in our own lives, and we expect to bequeath it to posterity for ever. We are also aware that you, like everyone else, would do as we are doing had you at your disposal the forces which are at ours. So much for the favour of heaven. As for Sparta, if you imagine she will assist you from a sense of honour, we can but admire your innocence;

we do not envy your folly. Sparta is a country of high moral standards in home affairs: its loyalty to national institutions is very great. Of its foreign policy we could say a good deal. Suffice it now to state that it is second to none in identifying national interests with national honour, national expediency with international justice.

"The Athenians left the conference: the Melians after consultation resolved to persevere in their refusal to surrender. The Athenian delegation then returned to the army and the generals immediately commenced hostilities. Later on, Melos was closely besieged and whispers of treachery began to be heard in the city. She therefore made an unconditional surrender to Athens. The Athenians executed all the men and enslaved all the women and children. They repopulated the island with five hundred colonists."

Thucydides did not pretend that this was a verbatim account of the negotiations at Melos, or that Athenian statesmen ever talked in this way. It is doubtful indeed if any of them had analysed their own motives or thought out the principles of their foreign policy so carefully as the cool objective spectator. The Melian Dialogue is not literal history, but an attempt to lay bare the real underlying causes of Athenian imperialism and to show what an Athenian diplomatist would have had to say if he had been honest enough to think out the implications of his country's policy. It is certain that Socrates would regard the Melian dialogue as a fair analysis.

Thucydides was an historian: he stated the facts

and analysed them without drawing any conclusions. But there were men at Athens prepared to draw them, and to assert not only that Athenian foreign policy was ruthlessly imperialistic but that it was *right* to be so. This school of *Realpolitik* was never a popular movement (it was too philosophical for that), but it deeply influenced the young intellectuals and its slogans were quickly picked up by the demagogues and popular lecturers. It maintained (as its modern counterparts maintain) that all politics are and must be power-politics: state against state, class against class, man against man. The survival of the fittest is the only law of human society, and self-interest the only motive of individual men. Not only inter-national law and morality, but social morality as well, are tricks and devices for the enslavement of one group by another. The position is admirably summarized by *Callicles*, a character whom Plato introduces in his dialogue the *Gorgias* to represent the philosophy of the younger generation.

"I believe that the laws are framed by the weak and common crowd. They frame them for their own benefit and according to their taste they concoct the code of moral praise and censure. They use them to terrify the few dominant spirits who could stake out a decent claim for themselves: to prevent them from doing well or getting the better of their inferiors. They are content with a fair or just distribution of wealth precisely because they are inferior. And so, Law tells us, it is unfair and disgraceful to try to do better than the common herd, and they tell us it is morally wrong to do so. But the real truth is that the better man ought to do better than the worse, and the more capable than the less capable. There is plenty of evidence to support this. Look at the behaviour of animals, look at the history of cities and of nations. Here you see Right means that the strong should rule the weak and do better than the weak. What right had Xerxes to attack Greece? I believe Xerxes and his like were doing what is really and truly right; they were acting by the real law of nature, though they may well have been transgressing the laws we frame. We take the finest of our children and we tame them like lion cubs, curbing their spirits with moral spells and superstitions. And so we enslave them, telling them they must only take their fair and proper share and that fairness and justice are what is fine and right. But if a man should arise with a spirit great enough for the task, he would shake off all this morality: he would burst the chains of convention and make himself free: he would trample underfoot our codes and hypocrisies and superstitions and all our unreal laws. The slave would rise up and show himself to be our master and true righteousness would shine forth."

This type of argument was as common in fifth-century Athens as it is to-day, and then, too, it seemed overwhelmingly persuasive to a generation which had grown impatient of the catchwords and speeches of democracy. Socrates must have heard it almost daily, and recognized in its triumphant despair of human nature a genuinely revolutionary tone. The young men who revelled in their immorality and denounced human kindness as a fraud were largely justified in their contempt for current morality. Socrates agreed with them that imperialism and class-war were the two main elements in the politics of their day. He agreed that most people in their private lives were moral and decent and righteous only because and so long as it paid them to be so: they kept their promises, paid their debts and fulfilled the laws from a mixture of fear and habit and common sense. And finally he agreed that at bottom the respectable citizen was often actuated by the same motive as Callicles—self-interest: the one accepted and the other renounced the social code, but the motive of self-interest was the same in both cases. But though he agreed with the *Realpolitiker* thus far, he parted company with them when they went on to affirm not only that men *did*, but that they *should* behave in this way. For here he saw the difference between philosophical and sophistical education. The former was concerned to find a new self-discipline based on rational moral principles: the latter regarded all morality as a brake on individual freedom. To Socrates the philosophy that might is right was the inevitable result of neglecting true philosophy and allowing education to fall into the hands of irresponsible Sophists. Class conflict and imperialism had dominated Athenian life because genuine philosophy had never been taught: and now a spurious philosophy had arisen designed to preserve precisely those evils which philosophy should suppress. *Realpolitik* was, in fact, the philosophy of Unreason, the justification of those false educational ideals which regarded knowledge and reason as merely useful instruments for the furtherance of personal or class-interests.

Socrates opposed this new philosophy of Unreason as firmly as he opposed the Sophists, and many of his fiercest arguments were directed against it. But the tide was against him. In a period of open class-war it seemed a hopeless task to educate Athens to moral and intellectual self-discipline: it was self-evident that in order to survive man must be prepared to fight for himself and disregard the obligations which reason and common decency alike imposed. The philosophy of Unreason at least offered a positive solution of the problems of life. It was concrete, specific, and "true to life." In opposition to it Socrates could offer nothing clear-cut or definite; his whole philosophy forbade him to teach a dogma. He could only try to put others on their way upon the search for truth. He could show that in the long run "Might is Right" is self-destructive, and that the philosophy of Unreason is the denial of all philosophy: but this was of little use to a generation filled with scepticism and despair.

For this reason Socrates' philosophy could make no headway against *Realpolitik*. Its simple patriotism and sense of duty sounded archaic and naïve, and its refusal to offer a ready-made solution of any problem made it seem nebulous and unworldly. But to the outsider Socrates and his opponents were much of a muchness. For up to a point both philosophies had a common aim, the exposure of hypocrisy; and where they differed—in the positive side of their teachings—Socrates' views were obscure and vague.

Thus the two conflicting educational ideals were lumped together by the ordinary Athenian as the clever revolutionary propaganda of aristocratic intellectuals whose purpose was the corruption of the youth and the destruction of all respect for the democratic tradition. This judgment may have been strictly incorrect, but it showed a certain political common sense. For, in fact, the products of Socrates' teaching were not distinguishable from those of the Sophists. Alcibiades was an unprincipled careerist, Critias a sadistic and ruthless politician. Looking at them the man in the street could not be blamed for assuming that Socratic philosophy was only another brand of subversive sophistry.

To appreciate, therefore, the tragedy of Socrates' execution, we must realize that it was politically justifiable. The statesman must consider the results of a policy or a creed, and not the motives which inspire it. Looked at from this point of view, Socrates' guilt was proved up to the hilt. His teaching had inspired the counter-revolution, and his theology had produced, not a puritan revival, but a ruthless and cynical gang of wealthy adventurers. The fact that he had denounced their philosophy of force did not make any material difference. His disciples had welcomed his attacks on current morality, and disregarded the positive side of his creed.

The responsibilities of the teacher are great. He must consider not only whether his teachings are true, but what effect they will have on his pupils. In the eyes of the practical politician it is no justification of Socrates as a teacher to show that he denounced wickedness, if his virtuous teachings, in fact, promoted it. However blameless his life and pure his motives, the effects on Athenian life had been disastrous. When we remember this, we cannot blame the jury which found him guilty of corrupting the youth.

We have seen how Socrates failed to impart to his pupils the rational self-discipline which he himself practised, and we have suggested that this failure was due to his inability to give any positive content to his notion of Reason which was acceptable to an Athenian audience. And yet Socrates had a positive gospel: and it was this gospel which was attacked in the second part of his charge which accused him of worshipping strange gods.

Here, too, we are faced with a paradox. Socrates was a respectable Athenian. There is no reason to believe that he was ever blasphemous or disrespectful to Athena of the Acropolis. How, then, could he be condemned upon this charge? From all that we hear of him, there is no doubt that he was a deeply religious man. He often talked of his "inner voice" which would suddenly forbid him to do something which he had in mind, and he believed that on those occasions God had spoken. He was something of a mystic and would sometimes fall into trances. Once when he was serving in the army in Northern Greece, he was observed in the early morning standing quite still meditating. There he stood all day deep in thought. As night fell some of his fellow soldiers dragged their beds out into the open to watch him.

All night he stood there quite still, and with the return of light he offered up a prayer to the sun and went on his way.

The inner voice and the trances were the most obvious signs of a religious sense which permeated Socrates' whole life. Religion for most Greeks at this time was a matter of *observance* and ceremony. Piety and godliness meant doing a number of things at the proper time; for the gods were "powers" to be appeased by offerings. The respectable citizen made his offerings, but religion did not demand that he should behave in any special way in his ordinary life, or offer him any very cheerful prospect in the next world. Greek gods were capricious and somewhat mercenary—a bad man, who made the proper offerings, was pleasing to heaven: a good man, who by some mischance failed to make them, was punished.

Socrates' religion was very different. All his life he had a mystical awareness of the supernatural world, and felt himself a citizen of the heavenly city. This other-worldly belief was held by certain sects called Orphics, which had grown up during the fifty years before he was born. For the Orphic human life was a vale of woe to which man had been banished by God, and the body was a tomb in which the immortal soul had been imprisoned. To gain true happiness it must be freed from the trammels of the flesh, and return to its natural dwelling-place in heaven. But this release could only be achieved if it renounced wealth and power and bodily pleasure and resolved to live the good life here on earth.

All men alike, said the Orphic, are banished souls,

so all are brothers. Cities and empires and earthly glory are nothing but vanity. We must renounce them and renounce our citizenship of this world. For the community of the elect is not bound by ties of kinship or of nationality, but by the brotherhood of its common purpose—its resolution to escape the world and "practice immortality," to subdue the flesh and seek God. Thus for the Orphic religion was no mere formal observance or empty ritual, but the very life of man. And his morality in the same way ceased to be the customs of the city he lived in, and became the way of life which the individual soul must follow if it is to be freed from the prison of the body and return to heaven.

Orphism often degenerated into a mystery cult hawked round by quacks and mendicants as a cheap ticket to heaven. But Socrates met the very exalted form of it which had been developed by the Pythagoreans. As it permeated their mathematics and made of them not merely a new science or technique, but a new theology, so it permeated his new dialectical analysis of the meanings of words and gave to it a strange passion and intensity.

"Perhaps, then, there is a 'narrow way' which leads us to our goal. For as long as we have the body with us in our search, so that the soul is contaminated by its evilness, we shall never get complete possession of that truth which we desire. The body must be fed, and so it constantly disturbs us. It is liable to disease and so it hinders our search for reality. It fills us with passions and appetites and fears and all sorts of phantasies and foolishness so that it really never gives us a chance of knowing anything properly. War and dissension and battle are all due to the body and its appetites, since every war is fought in order to acquire wealth, and it is the body which forces us to acquire it. And so we are enslaved to its service, and are so busy that we have no time for philosophy. But, worst of all, if the body *does* ever give us a little spare time and we begin to make some investigation, it constantly butts in, in the middle of our research, and disturbs and upsets us, and prevents us from seeing the truth. It is, in fact, obvious that if we are to gain any pure knowledge, we must get rid of the body so that the soul by itself can look on reality by itself. Only then shall we attain that knowledge which must be the object of our desire, since we claim to be 'lovers of knowledge.' Our argument proves indeed that we shall never know in this life, but only when we are dead. . . .

"The true philosophers really practice dying and they are less afraid of death than anyone. Look at it in this way. They are at logger-heads with the body and they want to free the soul of all encumbrances. Wouldn't it be very unreasonable then if they were afraid and upset when this happened, and were sorry to go to the place where there is a hope of gaining what they longed for all through their lives, and of ridding themselves of the companion with whom they were always at logger-heads? Many have been glad to die when the boy or wife or son whom they loved has been taken from them, simply because they hoped in the other world to see those whom they longed for and to be with them again. And so, I suppose, if a man is in love with knowledge and passionately believes that he cannot really find it except in the other world, he cannot be upset at dying, but will gladly leave this world. Surely this must be so if he is really a philosopher? For he will be passionately convinced that he can only find pure knowledge there. If this is so it would be very unreasonable for him to be afraid of death, wouldn't it?"

In this passage from the *Phaedo*[1] we find a clear statement of the Orphic religious faith. It can be summarized as follows: (1) The Soul is immortal. (2) Happiness means the achieving of immortality by renunciation of this world. (3) All men are brothers whatever their conditions here on earth. But to these three beliefs Socrates, under Pythagorean influence, adds a fourth—virtue is knowledge—transforming Orphism from a mystery cult into a rational philosophy. For now the immortal part of the soul is Reason, and happiness means freedom for Reason to contemplate reality. At one stroke the new scientific spirit becomes the instrument of true religion, and philosophical inquiry the proper method of theology, which alone can satisfy man's rational nature and impose upon his passions order and restraint.

At first sight it is not clear why Socrates' religion should have brought him into conflict with Athenian public opinion. Athens, too, had her own Eleusinian mysteries—a cult of Demeter and Persephone—which offered some hope of immortality, though it is doubtful whether the ordinary citizen regarded it as more than a kind of Freemasonry, a ceremonial

[1] *Phaedo*, chapters 11 and 12.

observance which satisfied a deep unconscious craving. Why, then, was Socrates condemned to death for worshipping strange gods?

There are several answers to this question. In the first place Pythagoreanism was an aristocratic creed, which challenged the sovereignty of the popular will and the authority of the elected citizen. In South Italy, indeed, a sort of dictatorship of the elect had been set up by Pythagoreans, like Calvin's City of God at Geneva. If knowledge must be supreme and reason control the passions, it was easy to see that the freedom which the merchants and town proletariat had won by a century of struggle would have to be surrendered to a stricter absolutism of theological kings. Athens rightly felt that the new puritanism was essentially undemocratic and that the Pythagorean, who was harmless enough when he confined his speculations to mathematics and the other world, would become a menace to the existing order if he applied his analysis to society. But this was precisely the task to which Socrates felt himself called—to use the new mathematical method of reasoning in testing the consistency and the correctness of the current morality and statesmanship. In so doing he must challenge the basic principles of Athenian democracy.

Secondly the Athenian was bound to ridicule the Socratic ideal of practising immortality. In a city where the pleasures of this world were so keenly appreciated, it seemed absurd to suggest that Puritanism could bring *happiness*. Socrates spoke constantly of the need to sacrifice all for *psyche*, the immortal

rational part of the soul. But to the Athenian the
psyche meant the breath of life; and if he conceived
it to be immortal, it was only as a thin shade in
Hades craving to return to the body. For him it was
the things of the body and of this world which
brought pleasure and made life worth living, and he
felt repelled by a doctrine which taught that man
must lose his life in order to save it.

Thirdly, the Socratic theology contradicted what
little religion he still had. Athena of the Acropolis
and the rest of the Olympic throng were for the new
theologians myths or allegories and nothing more.
The sun and moon and stars were physical objects
and studied as such by science. Homer, who was
almost a Greek bible, was mercilessly criticized and
the sexual foibles of his deities were denounced. It
was unreasonable to expect that the respectable citizen
should distinguish between a theologian who thus
trampled on tradition and a vulgar atheist. Socrates
for him was not only a Sophist and a crank—he was
blasphemous as well.

But all this is not sufficient to explain why Socrates
was brought to trial for his religious beliefs. Athens
was not a modern dictatorship and her citizens could
think what private thoughts they pleased. It cannot
have been Socrates' theology alone to which objection
was taken, but its political effects.

What these were it is easy to see. Socrates taught
that the religion which was ordinarily practised was
merely a myth, a symbol sometimes of truth, sometimes of falsehood. He believed that religion no less
than morality must be purged by reason and that,

before any real knowledge of God could be reached, the lumber of superstition and ceremony must be seen for what it was. In his own mind this exposure of superstition was only a preliminary before the real search for reality began. But for his pupils the preliminary stage was quite sufficient. They were delighted with his ridicule of Homer and all the sacred books of Greek morality. Rebels against tradition and orthodoxy, they wanted nothing better than a proof that religion was nonsense. Socrates gave it to them. Thus the effect of Socrates' teaching was not the restoration of true religion, but the destruction of any little religious feeling which Alcibiades and his friends still possessed; and the new theology had the same result in Athens as the new philosophy—it destroyed belief but was unable to put anything in its place. The young aristocrats may have picked up a smattering of Pythagorean teaching from their master, but they were only interested in its anti-democratic bias.

Socrates was the lover of truth who could only make men sceptics, the lover of God who converted his pupils to atheism, the patriot whose hearers became convinced that patriotism was a mere delusion. Preaching the rule of reason, he taught a technique of argument which was used to justify the rule of might. Concerned above all to challenge the selfish individualism of the Athenian intelligentsia, he produced by his teaching the worst specimens of that type.

Perhaps we can now understand why he refused to escape from prison and preferred to court death.

He knew that he had failed in his life to fulfil the mission which the Oracle had given him. He knew, on the other hand, that his teaching was sound and that along the way which he had marked lay the only hope of salvation for the individual and for the State. For his philosophy was not wrong, but incomplete. He preached the rationality of man and of God, and he urged that unless we believe in these two things there can be no sound education or happy society. His life had shown that this belief is insufficient and that without knowledge of the principles of human conduct, and of the nature of God, it can become positively harmful. But he believed that his death would inspire others to discover those things, the existence of which he could only take on trust.

We have said that it is the personality of Socrates, not his actions or teaching, which is really important. That he was justifiably condemned to death is true; but it is irrelevant to his greatness. That he made no important discoveries is also true and also irrelevant. What mattered to Plato and what matters to us is his life and death. In them he showed that a man could be found who believed so passionately in the cause of truth that he would follow it whatever its political or social effects. Such people there must always be if civilization is to be preserved. They are so uncompromising that they are quite unpractical: so simple that they make wise men look fools. Oblivious of the disastrous results of their idealism, they demand truth even where it may ruin a class or a city or a nation: and if their wickedness is pointed out to them, they merely reply, "where truth is concerned, compromise is impossible." All that is good in our Western culture has sprung from this spirit, whether it is found in scientists, or priests, or politicians, or quite ordinary men and women who have refused to prefer politic falsehoods to the simple truth. In the short term, they often do great harm: but in the end their example is the only force which can break the dictatorship of force and greed. Socrates was the first of these men and women of whose personality history has preserved a record.

For he was the first man who really saw what intellectual integrity implied and yet preferred it to everything else. He *was* the spirit of research, incorruptible, intolerant of sham, greedy for every variety of human experience, insatiable in discussion, ironic and yet serious. Such a spirit is generally intolerable to any well-organized community. The statesman who is responsible for "carrying-on," the priest who preaches the orthodox faith, the professor who repeats the traditional dogmas, will all unite to suppress the free spirit of reason which respects no authority save that of truth. In the face of completely candid criticism every established authority must resort to the most irrational of defences—force. There is no other weapon against the conscientious objector: and Socrates showed that philosophy is nothing else than conscientious objection to prejudice and unreason. Perhaps in the last resort it cannot solve the problems of human right and wrong, and it will have no simple answer to the questions of the hour. Regarding force as irrational, it will refuse to use it and ceaselessly demand that those who are prepared to do so should ask themselves precisely what their purpose and their motives are. The Athenian democracy had no answer to this question, and so Socrates died.

Socrates will always be compelled to die, his death will always be politically justifiable, and it will always be condemned by succeeding generations, who see so easily in retrospect that truth is ultimately preferable to any established falsehood, however efficient it may appear. Condemning the death of the historical Socrates, each generation kills its own.

4 PLATO

i. PLATO THE MAN

SOCRATES' execution was not in vain. By his death, like another conscientious objector four hundred years later, he immortalized the idea which he served; and the legend of Socrates became the inspiration of all who believe in reason. But the man who first formulated the Socratic faith into a systematic philosophy was fundamentally different from his master. Just as Paul of Tarsus created an orthodox Christian theology strangely remote in spirit from that of Jesus, so Plato modified the Socratic ideal of philosophy into a new Platonic system. Plato and Paul were both converts to a faith, but each of them changed the faith of his master almost as much as he was changed by it. And so in the history both of Platonism and of Christianity we find a strange tension between the ideals of the master and of the disciple; and at recurring intervals there is a movement to get behind the disciple's dogma to the real personality of the master. In the end loyalty to both is well-nigh impossible.

Consider for a moment these two men, Plato and Socrates. No two personalities could be more sharply opposed: Socrates, the humorous citizen of Periclean Athens, who knew and loved all sorts and conditions of men; Plato, the aristocrat, who shook the dust of democratic Athens off his feet: Socrates, the man who knew that he knew nothing; Plato, the systematic exponent of an authoritarian creed: Socrates, the conversationalist, and Plato, the master of prose style: Socrates, the personification of life itself, and Plato, the remote observer of all things living. It will be no surprise to find that the Socratic ideal under Plato's hand has suffered some startling transformations.

However long we study Plato's writings, we can never feel that we know Plato. He baffles and eludes our search, and although we may learn a good deal *about* him, to know or to like him as a man is almost impossible. This is due not only to his deliberate self-effacement in the dialogues—in his letters we possess extremely personal expressions of opinion—but also to his character. Plato was a divided personality, a man who deliberately denied himself full realization; a poet who deliberately allowed the springs of imagination to dry up. Unless we remember this we shall not grasp the full tragedy of his life. For he was first and foremost an artist, to whom practical affairs were of small interest. His poems are among the most exquisite we possess—and yet the story may well be true that the young Plato burned his tragedies and devoted himself to the cause of philosophy and of the regeneration of Greece. This decision was forced upon him by three things: his social position as a member of the ruling class who was naturally expected to devote his life to public service, the death of Socrates, which compelled him to see the urgency of the crisis, and lastly, the experiences of his youth.

Plato was born in 428. Pericles was dead: the great plague had ravaged Athens and the dreary years of the Peloponnesian war had just begun. Athens, connected by the Long Walls to her port, the Peiraeus, had become an armed camp into which each summer were huddled the Attic farmers, sheltering from the Spartan invasion and watching their crops burnt. Plato as a boy can have known little save war and the rumours of war, revolution and the rumours of revolution. War is never healthy for democracies, and as Plato grew up, Athens began to crack under the strain. As money ran short and the standard of living fell, the democratic leaders became more and more imperialist. In 430 Athens had been fighting to defend her Empire: by 416 it was necessary not only to repel attacks, but to recoup the losses of the war by some material gains—and Athens launched out on the enterprise of conquering Sicily, the richest island of the Mediterranean. The failure of the Sicilian expedition—caused in part by the defection of Socrates' favourite pupil, Alcibiades—meant the downfall of Athens, and in 404 she capitulated. Defeat in war brought revolution at home and an aristocratic terror was established. Plato was just twenty-four when this happened.

Belonging to one of the most distinguished families in all Athens, he had been brought up in an atmosphere of counter-revolution. In aristocratic circles, by this time, democracy was only another name for corruption and class-politics, and it was taken as self-evident that nothing but armed revolution could save her from collapse. Plato had never seen Periclean Athens: instead, he heard the savage jeers of the wealthy nobles at the inefficiency and vulgarity of the jingo democrats, and felt their growing terror of the uneducated proletariat with whom sovereignty lay. As the situation became worse, the cry for leadership grew louder, and at last the people itself began to tire of its freedom. The aristocratic politicians saw their opportunity, and Plato believed that the turning-point had now come; his friends would initiate the rule of Law and Order. Long afterwards, in a letter, he described his feelings in those troubled days: "My experience as a young man was by no means unusual. I thought that as soon as I became my own master I would immediately enter public life. A sudden change, however, in the political situation diverted me from my plan. The democratic regime of the time was generally detested and a revolution took place. It was headed by fifty-one leaders, of whom eleven were in the City and ten in the Piraeus: these two committees dealt with the market and with the administration of the two towns. Above them was a supreme committee of thirty. Some of the members of this supreme committee were relations or acquaintances of mine and invited me to join them, imagining that I should find the new regime to my taste. My feelings were in no way surprising if you consider my age at the time. I thought the new regime would substitute the reign of justice for the reign of injustice, and so I gave it my closest attention to see what it would do. And I saw these gentlemen within a very short time make the democracy they had destroyed seem like a golden age! They actually ordered my aged friend Socrates, whom I would not hesitate to call the most upright man of his time, to take part in the arrest of a citizen whom they wished to put out of the way. Their intention was to associate Socrates, whether he wished it or no, with the activities of the new regime. He refused to obey and was prepared to face death rather than be made an accessory to their crimes.

"When I saw all this and a good deal else besides, I was deeply disgusted and dissociated myself entirely from this deplorable government. Shortly afterwards, the thirty were turned out and their whole regime destroyed. Once again I was really, though less urgently, filled with a desire to take an active part in politics. Athens was still very unsettled and revolting incidents were not uncommon. It was not surprising that those revolutionary times resulted in personal reprisals of a violent character: but on the whole the restored democracy exercised considerable moderation. And yet, as ill-luck would have it, certain influential persons brought an action against Socrates. The charge was an outrageous one, of which Socrates was completely innocent. They accused him of impiety, and on this count the jury condemned to death the man who previously, when some of them had the misfortune to be in exile themselves, had refused to take part in the arrest of one of their own friends.

"When I considered all this, the type of men who were administering affairs, and the condition of the Law and of public morality—the more I considered it and the older I grew, the more difficult appeared to me the task of decent government. It was impossible to take action without friends or political associates, and these it was not easy to find among the politicians, since their methods of government were false to the true principles and traditional institutions of our country. To find new men for the job, however, was an impossibility. Moreover, statutes and usage alike were degenerating in Athens with surprising rapidity, and so, although at first I was filled with an ardent desire to enter politics, when I considered all this and saw how chaotic the political situation was, I felt completely baffled. I continued to consider how on earth some improvement could be brought about, not only in the administration, but also in society as a whole, and I was constantly on the look-out for an opportunity to intervene. But finally I came to the conclusion that every city without exception is badly governed, and that the state of legislation is everywhere so deplorable that no government is possible without drastic reconstruction combined with some very good luck. And so I was forced to extol true philosophy and to declare that through it alone can real justice both for the State and for the individual be discovered and enforced. Mankind (I said) will find no cessation from evil until either the real philosophers gain political control or else the politicians become by some miracle real philosophers."[1]

It is clear from this quotation that the shortcomings of the anti-democratic revolution were the first great disappointment of Plato's life: they shook him out of his complacency and made him reconsider his whole position. Up till now he had assumed that everything

[1] See Plato, Letter VII.

could be put right if only the gentlemen gained control. Now he realized that "the gentlemen" could behave worse than the demagogues of the proletariat. But this did not alter his profound contempt for the working population. Plato remained an aristocrat, convinced that the peasant, the craftsman, and the shopkeeper were incapable of political responsibility. Government was the perquisite of the gentry, who did not need to earn a living and could therefore devote their lives to the responsibilities of war and politics. In the eyes of the young Plato there must always be a ruling aristocracy and a subject people. The latter were the producers and distributers of material wealth, and Plato had a special word, "banausic," to express his contempt for their menial occupations. The former had the paternal care of the state at heart. Living on the labour of the subject masses, they gave them in return security, justice, and defence. Because they were of a nobler breed, culture and education belonged to them, while to the subjects was allotted that technical training which would best increase their efficiency as craftsmen or farmers. The political philosophy of the young Plato was at bottom a longing to return to the Homeric age of chivalry. Drawn from his reading of the *Iliad*, it postulated a radical reconstruction of the social order. The working classes must be put in their place: the gentry must regain their old self-confidence and sense of responsibility.

The failure of the anti-democratic revolution did not profoundly alter Plato's view: it merely proved that the reconstruction could not come through the normal political channels. A discredited aristocracy could never win power at Athens: but this did not prove that aristocracy as such was wrong. Somehow, on Plato's view, the gentry must be trained to play their proper part. How that was to be done he did not know, and was content for the moment to devote himself to mathematics and pure philosophy, and to discussions with Socrates, his master and friend.

Then came the trial and the death of Socrates. It is noteworthy that Plato did not lay it to the charge of the restored democracy, but admitted that the new government acted with considerable moderation. He saw, indeed, that it was one of those events which no foresight or human volition could have prevented. But because it could happen under a moderate democracy, it disturbed him profoundly. For years he had talked with Socrates and studied with him the new science and mathematics and theology: more than most of his contemporaries he had understood the Socratic spirit. He had not failed to see Socrates' deep disgust with the aristocratic clique and his contempt for their *Realpolitik*. He had grasped the reason for his refusal to escape from prison, and seen him as he was, not an agnostic, but a conscientious objector. Now that he was dead, Plato felt himself alone, but he also felt that his vocation was clear. He must overcome his deep revulsion from politics and do what Socrates had failed to do. He must answer the questions which Socrates asked, and discover those eternal principles of human conduct which alone could bring happiness to the individual and stability to the State. He must use the Socratic dialectic not only to discredit hypocrisy and false pretensions, but to reveal what real justice and courage and temperance are, and then work out a constitution and a system of law consistent with them. And lastly, he must build a city-state so firmly based upon reason and truth that Socrates, the conscientious objector, could have given it his wholehearted approval and loyalty, and lived with a good conscience under its protection. For Socrates' death, he believed, could only be made good if it inspired his friends and disciples to devote themselves to this one task.

Throughout his life Plato regarded himself as the fulfilment of Socrates. Because he believed this, he wrote the Dialogues and made no attempt to show where Socrates speaks in his own name and where he is the mouthpiece of Plato. Any such distinction would have seemed unreal to the man who had grasped the meaning of Socrates' life. Reason and truth are not the trappings of individual personalities: they are eternal and universal, and in them individual differences disappear. So at least both Plato and Socrates believed, and therefore the distinction of the real from the Platonic Socrates was for Plato absurd. Devotion to his memory would encourage Plato to a meticulous recreation of the world in which Socrates lived and talked, but not to a rigid separation of the master's philosophy from his own.

In his written works Plato tried to give flesh and blood to the Socratic spirit, the spirit of philosophy, The Dialogues are not dogmatic assertions of truth, but examples of philosophy at work, exposing falsehood, asserting new principles, finding fault again with these new principles and ascending ever higher in search of laws completely acceptable to reason. For Plato, the dialogue was the proper medium of philosophical thought because it displayed in its very form the fact that truth can only be found by *co-operation*; and—up to the time when he wrote the *Republic*—the Socratic dialogues were his only written work because Socrates was for him the supreme embodiment of this method.

It is impossible in one short chapter to solve a problem argued by scholars for hundreds of years. The relation of Plato to Socrates is a problem of this sort, but it is doubtful whether much of the argument has been of profit. Plato was no Boswell devoted to the immortalization of a Johnson far greater than himself. On the other hand his Socrates was not a fiction behind which his own personality was screened. If we look for analogies, we shall find one not in the writer of the Fourth Gospel, but in St. Paul. The Fourth Gospel is the work of a contemplative and placid mind. The dialogues are as fiercely controversial and pugnaciously loyal as Paul's epistles. Both writers feel themselves so immersed in the mission of the men whom they describe that it is difficult to separate what was original from the added touches. Socrates was an individual whom Plato had loved and whose memory he wished to perpetuate, but he was also the founder of a movement far greater than himself, which Plato believed himself to have developed upon true Socratic lines, but far beyond the point which Socrates had reached. For this reason the Socrates of the dialogues is at the same time the historical Socrates and the timeless spokesman of Platonic philosophy. Plato saw no inconsistency in this.

But writing was not enough. Socrates had demanded not only the discovery of truth, but its embodiment in human society: the double demand must be ful-filled, and Plato decided to prepare himself for the task. He could not now renounce politics and find consolation in poetry or in pure philosophy, although every natural inclination urged him to do so. Science and mathematics must, if Socrates were right, be harnessed in the cause of Greek regeneration: they must not be allowed to become a way of escape for an *intelligentsia* grown weary and anxious to avoid its civic responsibilities. Plato must have been greatly tempted by the claims of pure speculation. It was as easy for him as for the modern academic to pretend that truth alone was his objective, and that its appli-cability in the real world was not and should not be the concern of the pure scientist or philosopher: that theory and practice were rightly divorced from one another and that the former should be proud of its remoteness from everyday life.

There are many passages in the Dialogues in which Plato expresses his distaste for practical life[1] and extols the virtues of academic research. But always on such occasions an element of self-justification is apparent. The well-born recluse tries to rationalize his hatred of the mob into a theory of human stupidity.

[1] See particularly the *Phaedo* and the *Theaetetus* (172).

The academic, distrusting his political capacities, demonstrates the triviality of politics. But the apologia is always uneasy. Plato could never devote himself to metaphysics without feeling the prick of conscience reminding him that metaphysics were an escape from life. In the *Republic* (496) he says: "There is only a handful left who are inspired by the true spirit of philosophy, among them perhaps a man of noble character who was brought up in a good home and was saved from corrupting influences by banishment, and so has remained true to his own nature: or a great personality born in a small city who despises the petty politics of his home town and can therefore see beyond them.

"Those who become members of this small company and have made philosophy their own, realize the pleasures and the blessedness which it brings and appreciate fully the madness which has taken possession of the masses. They all know that to all intents and purposes nothing sound is ever achieved by the politicians, and that no one who tries to uphold justice will find any support on which he can rely. He will indeed be like a man who has fallen into a den of beasts, refusing to accept the law of the jungle but unable by himself to hold out against a bestial world: and so, before he can do anything for the city or his friends, he is put away, and a life is wasted without profit to himself or anyone else.

"Considering all this coolly and objectively, the philosopher will remain quietly at his own work, like a traveller caught in a storm who retreats behind a wall to shelter from the driving gusts of dust and hail. Seeing the rest of the world filled full with iniquity, he will be content to keep his own life here on earth unstained by wickedness and impious actions, so that he may leave this world with a fair hope of the next, at peace with himself and God." This streak in Plato's character is never wholly absent from his writings. It accounts for his ignorance of human nature—the natural superior can rarely understand the mob which he despises—and also for the uncertainty which runs through his whole career as to the purpose and direction of his researches and teaching. Later moralists and philosophers have shown the same defect—an inclination to forestall criticism of practical failure by saying in advance, "I'm willing to try my hand at putting the world to rights: but if my suggestions fail, I take no responsibility since my real interest is in pure theory."

It was the influence of Socrates which saved Plato from renouncing practical life. Socrates may have had a remote and mystical religion, but his intense interest in the world around him made it ridiculous even to suggest that he could take refuge in pure speculation. The fact that Socrates' feelings for Athens and his enjoyment of the life of the busy city had never wavered even in the face of death, was a constant reminder to Plato that a great teacher must also be a simple human being who loves and understands his fellow men. Plato could never be that, but at least he could apply the knowledge which he gained to the discovery of some cure for the miseries of his fellow men.

With these intentions, shortly after Socrates' death,

he left Athens and travelled for several years in the Mediterranean, probably visiting, among other places, North Africa, Egypt, and Sicily. He himself has recorded for us the impression which the first sight of the court of Dionysius I, Tyrant of Syracuse, produced upon him. "I was by no means content with the 'blissful life' which I found there, consisting, as it did, of incessant debauches. No one whose life is spent on gorging food twice a day and sharing his bed at night, and so on, could ever attain real wisdom. The human constitution cannot stand the strain of that sort of life for long. Nor would he ever be likely to learn self-control or any other virtue. What is more, no State, however good its laws, can retain any stability if its citizens believe in mad extravagance and exert themselves only in the activities of eating and drinking and in the vigorous pursuit of their amours. Inevitably in such a state there is a constant succession of tyrannies, oligarchies, and democracies; and the politicians cannot endure the mention of just government or equality before the law."

This visit to Sicily and South Italy was to prove of great importance in Plato's development. In the first place he became acquainted with Archytas, the geometer, who was trying to apply Pythagorean principles to the government of his native city Tarentum. Here Plato could see realized in a wealthy Italian town his dream of the rule of reason, and the sight must have encouraged him in his own designs. In the second place, in Syracuse, he met Dion, the son-in-law of Dionysius I, and immediately struck up a close friendship with him. A statesman of great practical ability, Dion was for Plato the ideal man of action. A passionate student of philosophy, he was willing to submit himself to the Platonic discipline and was later to become an ardent pupil in the Academy. But, above all, he was the *friend* of Plato; the two seemed to be complementary to each other, the politician with a bent for philosophy and the philosopher driven by his conscience into the practical world. After Socrates, Dion was the most important influence in Plato's life.

At the age of forty Plato returned to Athens to see in 387 the conclusion of the ignominious peace of Antalcidas by which all Asia Minor was surrendered to Persia. Hellenic independence was ebbing, but the old feud between Sparta and Athens still continued and Athens had won back something of the glories of the empire from her rival. Plato, however, had made his decision. Athens offered him no prospects and so in a shady garden outside the walls he founded his new university—the Academy.

The Academy was both a school and an institute of scientific research. There, for the first time, the two sides of modern university life were joined together. Visited by nearly all the famous scientists of the time, it soon ceased to be an Athenian institution and became one of the centres of Greek learning. The students, too, were by no means exclusively from Athens, but included the sons (and daughters!) of some of the most distinguished families in Greece. Plato renounced Athenian politics to become the president of the first pan-Hellenic university. In a later chapter we shall see something of the educational system which he proceeded to build up: at present we are only concerned to observe the double purpose of the Academy, on the one side as an organization for pure research, and on the other as a training ground for young men of the leisured classes (and mostly of noble blood) who were destined to a political career in their home cities. Here, at last, Plato had found a field for practical activity which was not confined to Athenian party-politics: here he could build up a community of young disciples and imbue them with the moral and intellectual discipline which was necessary if they were to restore the ancient glories of Greece. In the pure air of the Academy they could throw off party and factional interests and avoid the corruption of life in the degenerate city-state. Steeped in the spirit of philosophy, they would become leaders of a new and purer Hellenism and carry back with them to their homes the revolutionary creed of the Academy.

For twenty years Plato was content to guide the policy of the new university, and in a series of Socratic dialogues to indicate the lines along which its research should be conducted. But in 367, when he was close on sixty, an event happened in Sicily which was to provide the philosopher with a test of the practical utility of his work. Dionysius I of Syracuse died and was succeeded by his son, Dionysius II. The latter, a young man of thirty, was not a strong character and his education, or lack of it, had done little to improve his natural capacities. For this reason Dion became the power behind the throne and suggested to the new tyrant that Plato should be invited to undertake his education and to advise him on general policy. The invitation was given and Plato set sail for Sicily.

We need not carry the story of Plato's life further;[1] for it is the Plato of 367 B.C. whom we have decided to confront with the problems of our modern world. It is clearly impossible to ask what Plato would think to-day without specifying more precisely which Plato we mean, the young disillusioned politician, the middle-aged president of the Academy, serenely certain of the power of philosophy to rule the world, or the old man, sceptical and cautious, who composed the *Laws*. It is the second of these whom we have chosen, and for this reason we shall take as representative of his thought the famous dialogue called the *Republic*, which he composed some years before his journey to Sicily. The *Republic* was not only the manifesto of the Academy, but also the programme of the philosopher statesman, and if we read it carefully, we can observe many indications that it was composed with the possibility of an invitation from Syracuse constantly in view. It has, therefore, a peculiar appropriateness to our present task, since it discusses all the main philosophical problems, with reference to practical political questions.

ii. PLATO'S PROGRAMME OF POLITICAL REFORM

The *Republic* is Plato's plan for the building of a perfect state in which every citizen is really happy. He imagines himself invested with supreme power

[1] For some account of Plato's later life see Chapter 10.

and asks how he would use it to save humanity from its present miseries. But if you are going to build a perfect society, you can only do so by reconstructing existing institutions; and so Plato was forced to consider the city which he knew so well, and to ask himself what was wrong with Athens. When he had discovered this, he could construct a city free from the evils of Athenian society.

Plato believed that these evils were three in number: class-war, bad government, and bad education. Class-war was the most obvious of the three. Most Greek cities were either oligarchies or democracies and many alternated through a series of revolutions between these two forms of class dictatorship. In the former political power was held by an alliance of landowners and merchants, with the support of the farmers and peasants: in the latter the leaders of the town proletariat moulded policy with the uneasy support of certain commercial interests. In both the opposition was ruthlessly fleeced. The effect of the Peloponnesian war had been to intensify the political struggle. It has been described by Thucydides in a famous passage.[1]

"The whole Greek world was convulsed by the great war. In each city the democratic politicians called on Athens to assist them in their domestic conflict, while the oligarchs relied on Sparta. In peace time they would have had no justification and no desire for foreign intervention; but in war the weapon of alliance was ready to hand. Each side could use it for its own benefit and for the destruction of its

[1] *Thucydides*, III, 82.

opponents, and intervention could be employed by anyone who was plotting a *putsch*. Revolution brought those horrors to the cities of Greece which will always recur so long as human nature is unchanged, and which vary in their intensity and character according to the variations of the social conditions. In peace time and in prosperity state and individual alike are actuated by higher motives, because they are not faced with inevitable choices. But war destroys the comfortable routine of life, schools us in violence and adapts our character to the new conditions. . . . The cause of all these evils was imperialism, whose fundamental motives are ambition and the acquisitive instinct, and from which arises the fanaticism of class-conflict. The politicians on each side were equipped with high-sounding slogans: the Left claimed that they were the champions of the constitutional rights of the people, the Right that they stood for aristo-cracy, law, and order. Both boasted that they were devoted servants of the community and both made the community the prize of war. The only purpose of their policy was the extermination of their oppo-nents, and to achieve this they flinched from nothing. Even worse were the reprisals which they per-petrated in total disregard of morality or of the common good. The only standard which they recognized was party caprice, and so they were pre-pared, either by the perversion of justice or by revolutionary action, to glut the passing passions engendered by the struggle. Religion was respected by neither: they preferred to applaud the use of fair phrases for the achievement of odious ends. Between

H

them the middle class was wiped out, either because they refused to participate or because neither side could bear to let them survive.

"Thus class-conflict produced every form of evil in the Greek world. Simplicity, which is an essential element in true nobility of character, was ridiculed and disappeared. Society was divided into warring camps, suspicious of one another. Where no contract or obligation was binding, nothing could heal the conflict, and since security was only to be found in the assumption that nothing was secure, everyone took steps to preserve himself and no one could afford to trust his neighbour. On the whole the baser types survived best. Aware of their own deficiencies and their opponents' abilities, they resorted boldly to violence, before they were defeated in debate and struck down by a conspiracy of minds more versatile than their own; whereas the more intelligent, confident that they could anticipate the others' plans and that it was unnecessary to use crude methods where subtle policy was possible, were taken off their guard and so destroyed."

To the modern ear, attuned to the horrors of the Spanish revolution, Thucydides' analysis needs no explanations. The breakdown of established law, caused by the great war, had in his day, as in ours, intensified the class-struggle, and destroyed the possibility of peaceful change or constitutional government. Violence had become the only weapon in the struggle for survival, and dictatorship the only organization to ensure economic interests. Plato realized that, unless the class-war could be ended,

Greek culture could not long survive. But between
the Left and the Right he, like Thucydides, found little
to choose. Both were actuated by selfish class interests:
both were willing to sacrifice the national welfare to
the immediate interests of their supporters. Both used
religion and morality as rhetorical devices for attaining their material ends. If there were any advantage,
it lay with the oligarchs, for their system was more
stable: because policy was concentrated in the hands
of a few, it was less likely to be swayed by gusts of
popular passion. On Plato's view the class-war, if it
were allowed to continue, could end logically only
in the destruction of all social life. For the qualities
necessary to survival were not decency or wisdom
or righteousness, but brutality and low cunning.

But if the class-war was the prime evil of Athenian
life, there were, in Plato's opinion, two other con-
tributory evils of great importance. The first was the
idea that government belonged by right to a particular social class *or* to the people as a whole. He
believed that it was a whole-time job and demanded
abilities of a peculiar kind. The State could only
prosper if political power were granted to men and
women who were capable of using it correctly. But
the oligarchs regarded government as the perquisite
of wealth, the democrats of citizenship, and so under
both parties the government was selected for reasons
which had little to do with its capacity for ruling.
The result was that in each case the machinery of
State became the instrument of class-interest: law
did not rule but was enslaved to a section of its own
subjects. It was on this score that Plato levelled his

most bitter attacks against Athenian democracy. The people claimed to govern themselves and proudly refused to submit the control of policy to any body of experts. Instead the citizen assembly itself made all important decisions. And what was the result? The people being incompetent, power fell into the hands of demagogues: and "ruling" became the perquisite not of the wise statesman, but of the mob-orator who knew how to cajole the people and to pander to its worst tastes.

"Conceive something of this kind happening on board ship, on one ship or on several. The master is bigger and stronger than all the crew, but rather deaf and short-sighted. His seamanship is as deficient as his hearing. The sailors are quarrelling about the navigation. Each man thinks that he ought to navigate, though up to that time he has never studied the art, and cannot name his instructor or the time of his apprenticeship. They go further and say that navigation cannot be taught, and are ready to cut in pieces him who says that it can. They crowd round the solitary master, entreating him and offering him every inducement to entrust them with the helm. Occasionally when they fail to persuade him and others succeed, they kill those others and throw them overboard, overpower the noble master by mandragora or drink or in some other way, and bind him hand and foot. Then they rule the ship and make free with the cargo, and so drinking and feasting make just such a voyage as might be expected of men like them. Further, they compliment anyone who has the skill to contrive how they may per-

suade or compel the master to set them over the ship,
and call him a good seaman, a navigator, and a
master of seamanship; any other kind of man they
despise as useless. They have no notion that the true
navigator must attend to the year and the seasons,
to the sky and the stars and the winds, and all that
concerns his craft, if he is really going to be fit to
rule a ship. They do not believe that it is possible for
anyone to acquire by skill or practice the art of
getting control of the helm, whether there is opposition or not, and at the same time to master the art
of steering. If ships were managed in that way, do
you not think that the true navigator would certainly
be called a star gazer and a useless babbler by the
crews of ships of that description?"[1]

This was Plato's picture of Athenian democracy—
a poor old skipper bullied, deceived, and cajoled by a
gang of knaves; and he believed that its desperate
plight was caused by its refusal to admit that law and
order are only possible if government is in the hands
of an *élite* specially trained for the task.

From this follows naturally his third criticism of
Athens. Education, which should be the major
responsibility of the State, had been left to individual
caprice and to the individual's capacity to pay. Here
again was a task which should be entrusted only to
the expert and to the man of proven probity. The
future of any State depends on the younger generation,
and it is therefore madness to allow the minds of
children to be moulded by individual taste and force
of circumstance. Equally disastrous had been the

[1] *Republic*, 488, Lindsay's translation.

State's *laissez-faire* policy with regard to teachers and schoolmasters and sophist-lecturers. It had allowed anyone who wished to earn his living in this way, whatever he taught. As a result the man in the street under the influence of irresponsible publicists, demagogues, and rhetoricians, had ceased to believe that such things as law or justice existed. The equalitarian philosophy which held that each man's opinion was as good as his neighbour's, had destroyed respect for authority and had turned democracy into licentious anarchy. Disregard of education was primarily responsible for this.

Faced by these three cardinal errors of Athenian democracy, Plato turned naturally enough—for he was an aristocrat—to Sparta. Here was a State which—apart from occasional serf revolutions—had maintained its social and political stability for two hundred years. Sparta had not avoided the class-war, but she had coped with it so successfully that she had escaped revolution. Plato saw that there were three reasons for this. In the first place, Sparta's economy was self-sufficient: she was an agricultural State with no imperial pretensions. In the second place, government there was in the hands of a specially trained hereditary ruling caste to whom the pleasures of wealth and luxury were forbidden; and lastly, in Sparta education was rigidly controlled by the State. Sparta had avoided all the evils of Athenian democracy, and Plato could not but admire her laconic austerity and her aristocratic contempt for commerce and self-government. His ideal State was to be framed on a Spartan model.

But his own political experience had shown him that Sparta was not the perfect State. To begin with, the ruthless suppression of serfs and the constant fear of revolution which accompanied it could not satisfy the idealist who wished to make every citizen happy. Plato dreamed of a civilized Sparta in which the serfs would be subjects, voluntarily submitting to the rule of law, not slaves terrorized by a secret police. But further, the Spartan ruling class had in his own lifetime demonstrated its own limitations. After 404 Sparta had succeeded to the Athenian Empire, and Spartan citizens had been sent out to administrate many of the towns once ruled by Athens. The results had been disastrous. Soldiers who had been used to barrack discipline and whose natural desires had been suppressed by rigid social tabus, found themselves in positions of irresponsible authority where they could do whatever they liked without let or hindrance. Alone on his island, the Spartan administrator suddenly discovered a new world of pleasures, and a new delight in giving, not receiving, commands. Like the public schoolboy in his first term at the university, he "let himself go," and within a few years the Spartan Empire was infamous for the cruelty and corruption of its administration. Once the individual was allowed to make money and enjoy the pleasures of self-expression, he discarded his aristocratic sobriety and military restraint and became a vulgar and brutal voluptuary: once the State discovered the pleasures of imperialism, it accepted them without any of its responsibilities.

Plato had seen this happen, and had realized that the cure for Athens was not simply a dose of Spartan tonic. Something else must be added, and he believed that this "something else" was to be found in the Academy.

For the Academy was designed to produce that spirit of disinterested research of which Socrates had been a living example. Its students were to become statesmen, who voluntarily submitted to the law of reason because they saw that this law was true and right. The Spartan boy had been taught the soldier's unreasoning submission to the commands of his superior. He had been "socially conditioned" to obey law, and for this reason, when he had to act on his own initiative and had no superior officer to control him, he could offer no resistance to natural desire. Just as "public school morality" often breaks down when the public schoolboy is isolated from his social class and can indulge himself in a whole gamut of forbidden pleasures without fear of disapproval, so Spartan militarism had failed to resist the temptations of imperial power. The Academy, however, provided just the university training which is supposed to turn a conventional public school morality into a reasoned and intellectual self-discipline: its products were not to be mere creatures of habit, but adult men with wills of their own, who understood the principles of law and decided voluntarily to obey them.

Thus while Sparta provided the foundations of the Platonic State, the Academy was to turn it from a tyranny into a benevolent dictatorship, which would rely not on sheer force, but on impartial government to retain the obedience of the subject class. The public schoolboy must be put under the command of the university graduate, his conventional morality controlled by the law of reason.

In the *Republic* Plato sketches the plan of a three-class State. At the top are the *philosopher kings*; then come the *administrators*, and below them both are all the *civilians*, who are unfit to rule themselves.[1]

And so we reach the famous proposition in which Plato summarized his whole political programme: "The city-state can only be saved if the kings become

[1] The words Plato used to describe his three classes are φιλοσοφοι (philosophers), ἐπικουροι (auxiliaries), and δημιουργοι (craftsmen), but the literal translations of the two latter are so misleading that I have avoided them in the text. Since Plato's lowest class includes all the population except the ruling *élite*, "working-classes" is as misleading a translation as "craftsmen," and I have finally decided on the word "civilian" to indicate the passive unpolitical nature of the third class. Plato's rulers are also soldiers, so that the word is not wholly amiss as long as it is clearly understood that its meaning is not exhausted in this contrast of soldier and civilian but must include also the contrast of "politically responsible" and "politically subject."

The substitution of "administrator" for "auxiliary" needs less defence. "Auxiliary" to the modern ear means precisely nothing: administrator at least gives something of the prime ideas of "active management" and "public service," and indicates the difference between the second class who are executive—at once the army and the civil service of the new State—and the first who are purely deliberative. Below these two, and carefully segregated from them, are the civilian masses, whose only civic duty is obedience to law, and abstention from all political activity. The Greek city-state is to be regenerated by Spartan discipline under the direction of the philosophic spirit of the Academy.

philosophers or the philosophers become kings."
Plato was convinced (as Socrates had been) that the
good State is the rational State, and that the good
ruler is the man who knows precisely the plan of
life which will give men happiness. The ruler must
understand the world he lives in, and the laws which
control it. He must know the science of politics as
clearly as the craftsman knows his special skill.
Ruling is not everybody's job. It is as specialized as
any other science or craft. We do not imagine that
anyone can attend us when we are ill, nor do we
elect our doctors democratically. We demand knowledge and experience of them, and we submit ourselves obediently to their commands. If we did not
we should suffer in health. Plato held that the same
was true of politics. The ruler must be as highly
trained as a doctor and he must be obeyed as im-
plicitly as we obey our doctor's orders.

But the doctor only looks after our bodily health
and he only attends us when we are ill. The ruler is
always with us: he must direct our whole lives, plan
our existence, and order our thoughts and emotions
as well as our bodies. Because he controls our whole
lives, his training must be more arduous and his
knowledge far wider than that of the doctor. The
ruler (in Plato's language, the philosopher-king) must
know the whole good for man and he must have the
character and resolution to impose it upon us without
stint. He must not be beguiled by our complaints or
tempted by our bribes. He must care about the plan
which he knows to be our salvation so much that he
can overlook the distress and pain which we shall

suffer, just as the doctor must neglect our suffering if
he is to save our life. In politics there are no anaesthetics
or drugs to make the suffering easier for the patient
to bear. For the good of the State the ruler must
punish and banish and kill the citizen who objects to
the political operation the State must undergo.

Thus the three-class State is really a two-class State
with a subdivision in the ruling class. The civilians are
the vast majority of the population, the peasants and
artisans and tradesmen who are engaged in the production and distribution of wealth. Their function is
to provide the material basis of social welfare, their
happiness to enjoy the just fruits of their labours
under the stable regime of law and order. Plato wastes
little time in discussing their organization, but he
assumes that his city will be economically self-
sufficient and will not depend on imports for the
necessities of life. Self-sufficiency will avoid the
need for imperialism and for the navy which[1] had
given political power in Athens to the urban worker.
In his city there will be no town-proletariat or
big-business or international bankers to upset the
natural harmony of economic interest. And so he
need not worry about the civilians since the economic
system will run itself provided that political power is
forbidden to the producer and distributor of wealth.
Class-conflict arose through the control of government by one vested interest: it is removed, according
to Plato, by allowing no vested interest whatsoever
to influence the government. By depriving every
economic interest of the means of oppression, he

[1] See page 36.

restores the natural identity of interest, creates the possibility of an impartial State, and so removes the possibility of oppression.

Once he has destroyed the power of the vested interests, a real aristocracy or *dictatorship of the best* is possible. From earliest childhood the ruling class is segregated from the civilians, and given a special education. They are to be gentlemen, unsullied by trade and the menial labours of agriculture and craftsmanship: and they are to follow the gentleman's calling of public service in the administration and the army. Whereas the civilian, with his vulgar interests in his craft, in money-making and in family-life, is a natural subject, the ruler, conscious of the social responsibility which higher intellectual and moral capacities bring, is a natural gentleman; and in Plato's State only the gentleman must rule. As children, these natural gentlemen are subjected to an iron discipline. Their fairy stories, their songs and their dances—all the influences which can mould their character—are censored and controlled. For they are to be the defenders of the State against internal discord and foreign aggression and on their absolute integrity depends the well-being of the whole community. Their education, therefore, is chiefly concerned to ensure three things. In the first place all personal interests must be suppressed, the desire for wealth, family, bodily pleasures, and so on. For such interests, if they become paramount in a ruler's life, will corrupt his administration and make him another wage-earner no better than the civilians. Plato's *élite* therefore must be given a moral training so strict and so severe that nothing can divert them from their service to the State. Secondly, they must be physically fit, and so they are brought up to a Spartan simplicity of diet and dress. For they are to be soldiers as well as administrators and they must be inured to military discipline from earliest childhood. Lastly, they must be given the rudiments of mental discipline. But their real intellectual education starts only at the age of twenty. Then they must concentrate for ten years upon higher mathematics and dialectic, until at thirty an examination is held in which future philosophers are selected.

Those who fail to pass this examination are the administrators proper, and it is their task to carry out the commands of the philosopher-kings. Unable themselves to become philosophers, they see that only obedience to philosophy will bring peace and security to men. Essentially men of action, ambitious for themselves and for the city, they have outgrown the petty pleasures of private life and find in public service their supreme happiness. Though they cannot themselves think creatively, they can apply the principles of philosophy once they are laid down, and their moral training has been such that nothing can divert them from this purpose.

The philosophers and the administrators live in barracks apart from the civilians. All military and civil power is in their hands, but they receive only a scanty wage from the subject population, and they are absolutely forbidden to have any contact with wealth. Owning nothing, they must guard the property of others, and they will do this faithfully only if their education has taught them to care for higher things. If a man wants wealth, he is not denied the fulfilment of his desire, but he must forfeit political power. Conversely, if he wants a life of public service, he is given the opportunity, provided that he renounces all interest in property. For it is only, on Plato's view, by the complete separation of political power from ownership of property that class-war can be abolished and the profit motive become the servant, not the tyrant, of society.

Plato believed that in a State reconstructed upon these lines, the happiness of every individual could be secured. Sacrifices are demanded from each class, but only to ensure the satisfaction of its dominant interest. By the surrender of political freedom, which has only brought him class-war, the civilian gains a stable regime in which rulers of absolute integrity will dispense justice, and well-trained soldiers will defend him from attack. He has lost his civil liberties, too, but he has no need of them, now that the social order is really just and impartial. For criticism is only necessary where rulers are corrupt: and the civilian is not the man to criticize since he has neither the knowledge nor the training to do so. The sacrifice of civil liberties, therefore, is the sacrifice of something which he was incapable of doing well and only undertook under the pressure of necessity. Apart from these losses—which many in Europe bear to-day with equanimity even when they are not blessed with the rule of philosopher-kings—his gains are enormous: in the first place, justice which is impossible under any other regime, in the second place, a certainty that his property will remain his own and that no one will take it from him. Plato believed that few men would ask for more.

The administrators will be happy too. Since their dominant interest is in government, and the driving motive of their life is ambition, they cannot but be content to hold in their hands the executive power of the State. After their early training they will not greatly miss the wealth which they must forgo, or even be upset by the law which forbids them to marry and have families;[1] for they are soldiers, inured to barrack life and to the sacrifice of personal pleasures for the sake of the common weal. As soldiers, too, they will be content on all decisive questions to obey the commands of the philosopher-kings—they know that they themselves do not know. Lastly, the philosophers will be happy, although they have the heaviest sacrifice to make. For their paramount interest is in research and yet they are compelled to spend much time and labour applying the results of their researches to the practical affairs of State. Plato had a natural sympathy with the few who could appreciate the life of "a scholar and a gentleman" and yet were forced to enter the political arena, and among British statesmen would have recognized in men like A. J. Balfour the characteristics of a true philosopher-king. It was men of this type alone that he chose for supreme political responsibility, hoping that a select band of Balfours would be able to relieve each other in rotation of the practical work for which they would all feel a justifiable distaste.

[1] See Chapter 7.

Such in barest outline was Plato's programme for the salvation of Greece—the restoration of the impartial rule of law through the dictatorship of the philosopher-kings. Only thus could the three evils of class-war, bad government, and bad education be cured and happiness provided for every citizen. The Academy must become not only the conscience but the political dictator of Greek society. In every city a Platonic scholar must be vested with absolute power.

There is no doubt that Plato faced the inevitability of the use of force for the achievement of these ends. His statesmen were to be trained soldiers with armies at their disposal, ready if necessary to meet force with force. But he believed that the extremes of violence could be avoided by education, and for this reason the *Republic* is silent on the subject both of how the philosopher is to attain power and of the details of political organization. We can, however,[1] fill in the gaps in the *Republic* from the history of Plato's and Dion's experiences in Sicily. Plato lived in aristocratic circles and his pupils were chiefly drawn from the sons of tyrants or leading aristocratic politicians. It seemed possible, therefore, that the 'dictatorship of the best' could be achieved without violent revolution if these young men could gain control in their respective cities. The Academy would then become the central advisory bureau of a network of aristocratic dictatorships, settling the general lines of policy on which each of the scholar-statesmen should proceed. It would be the headquarters of an "open conspiracy" to clean up Greek politics, the *Republic*

[1] See Chapter 10.

would be its manifesto and Plato the commander-in-chief.

This plan was no Utopian dream. Dion was a force in Sicilian affairs, Archytas in South Italy, and from many other cities came requests for Plato's advice and guidance. It seemed possible that the new university might really convert the rulers in non-democratic cities and make the kings philosophers. Plato disregarded the problem of how to capture power not because he was an unpractical dreamer, but because, in the revolution of which he dreamed, the capture of power would not prove difficult. He did not wish to turn out a ruling class, but to convert it. For this reason he paid little attention to the democracies, even to Athens. There he knew his chances were small. Only where an oligarchy or a military dictator was in control had he a real possibility of achieving his goal, since here political power was in the hands of a few men of his own social class.

The real problems, therefore, were firstly the conversion of the Greek gentleman to Platonic philosophy, and secondly the pacification of a proletariat avid for self-government. These are the practical questions which the *Republic* tries to answer, and both are in a sense educational. Of the first we have already spoken and we shall return to it in a later chapter. But the second is no less important. The civilian must be educated to accept his subjection to the rule of law. But since he is naturally incapable of philosophy or of directing his life according to reason and cannot understand the *raison d'être* of the State, it is useless to explain the truth to him. He must therefore be fed on political and religious myths, "noble lies" as Plato called them, which appeal to his emotions and stimulate him to obey the law.

By the "noble lie" Plato meant propaganda, the technique of controlling the behaviour of the stupid majority: and he believed that this was the only sort of general education which the civilian should receive. He must, in fact, be content with the education which Plato had prepared for the children of the ruling class, since politically and morally he would always remain a child. Just as children are told improving stories to prevent them from biting their nails or stealing or telling lies, so the civilian must be fed on propaganda to prevent him from asserting his right to self-government. One such story Plato himself suggested: "Yes," I said, "you are no doubt right; but still listen to the rest of the tale. 'You in this city are all brothers,' so we shall tell our tale to them, 'but God as he was fashioning you, put gold in those of you who are capable of ruling; hence they are deserving of most reverence. He put silver in the auxiliaries, and iron and copper in the farmers and the other craftsmen. For the most part your children are of the same nature as yourselves, but because you are all akin, sometimes from gold will come a silver offspring, or from silver a gold, and so on all round. Therefore the first and weightiest command of God to the rulers is this—that more than aught else they be good guardians of and watch zealously over the offspring, seeing which of those metals is mixed in their souls; if their own offspring have an admixture of copper or iron, they must show no pity, but giving

it the honour proper to its nature, set it among the
artisans or the farmers; and if on the other hand in
these classes children are born with an admixture of
gold and silver, they shall do them honour and
appoint the first to be guardians, the second to be
auxiliaries. For there is an oracle that the city shall
perish when it is guarded by iron or copper'."[1]

Philosophy for the ruler, and propaganda for the
rest—this, says Plato, is the best way of avoiding
bloodshed in the establishment and maintenance of
the 'dictatorship of the best.' The mistake of Socrates
had been his belief that the Law of Reason was suitable for everyone. He had condemned rhetoric and
sophistical education altogether and tried to convert
the city of Athens to philosophy. But philosophy
and reason are poison to the masses. Misunderstood
and perverted by them, they merely intensify social
unrest. The masses need not the truth, but a con-
venient falsehood. They, like Adam and Eve, must be
forbidden to eat of the Tree of the Knowledge of Good
and Evil—for their own sakes. The philosopher-king
therefore will not condemn propaganda altogether,
but will demand the absolute control of it by the
Government. Literature, music, religion, science—
everything which can disturb their minds must be
censored by the rulers and regulated so as to promote
the loyalty of the masses to the new regime. The
perfect State will be for the civilian quite literally
"a fool's paradise," controlled by a few wise men,
who out of their compassion for the masses provide

[1] *Republic*, 415, Lindsay's translation. For a striking modern
parallel compare Hitler's speech at the Nuremberg Rally in 1934.

them with superstitions and ceremonies and popular philosophies fit for their feeble capacities.[1]

Plato's philosophy is the most savage and the most profound attack upon Liberal ideas which history can show. It denies every axiom of "progressive" thought and challenges all its fondest ideals. Equality, freedom, self-government—all are condemned as illusions which can be held only by idealists whose sympathies are stronger than their sense. The true idealist, on Plato's view, will see men as they are, observe their radical inequalities, and give to the many not self-government but security, not freedom but prosperity, not knowledge but the 'noble lie.' The perfect State is not a democracy of rational equals, but an aristocracy in which a hereditary caste of cultured gentlemen care with paternal solicitude for the toiling masses.

Before the Great War, the *Republic* was often treated as the "Ideal State" which Plato never intended to put into practice. Its whole conception seemed far-fetched and remote to a generation which assumed Liberal ideas as self-evident truths of human nature. A world which believed that, under the flags of science, general education, and democracy, it was marching to perfection, could not swallow Plato's estimate of the common man, or seriously approve his educational programme. Unaware of the class-war, it could not understand his hatred of democracy and acceptance of dictatorship. But because Plato was a famous philosopher, he was rarely condemned outright as a reactionary resolutely opposed to every

[1] Cf. 'The Grand Inquisitor' in the *Brothers Karamazov*, where the same theory is worked out.

principle of the Liberal creed. Instead, he was elevated to a higher rank, and became an idealist, remote from practical life, dreaming of a transcendent City of God.

The war has changed all that. Plato's so-called "idealism" is now seen for what it is—a grimly realistic estimate of the moral and intellectual capacities of the masses. Knowing what class-war and revolution mean, we can understand why Plato advocated dictatorship to prevent them. Having some experience of the effects of propaganda, we can treat 'the noble lie' not as an amusing phantasy but as an extremely practical instrument of government. If we have any objection to Plato it is because he is too *COBBLERS* "realistic" in his analysis of human nature.

For this reason it is extremely pertinent to ask ourselves: "If Plato lived again, what would he make of our world, and what would we make of him?" His cure for the diseases of society are only too applicable to-day, and there are many who begin to feel "After all, if it *could* be done, it would be worth doing. Perhaps we have been building on foundations of sand. The ideals of freedom and democracy are crumbling away. Is it not better before it is too late to replace them with the Platonic 'dictatorship of the best'?" It is to such people that this book is addressed. For it tries to show how Plato fared in his own world, and how he would fare in ours.

5 PLATO LOOKS AT BRITISH DEMOCRACY

HAVING seen something of the world in which Plato lived and wrote, and of the plan which he put forward for its salvation, we are now faced with the infinitely more difficult task of transferring the Platonic plan to a modern setting and assessing its value there. At first sight it seems futile to ask what Plato would have thought of the nation-state or industrial democracy or the u.s.s.r. The whole scale of politics has been enlarged so vastly by our newly won control of nature that suggestions for the re-organization of the city-state must appear valueless to modern thinkers. There is a measure of truth in this. We cannot apply conclusions drawn from the study of one epoch to the problems of another, nor can we rely on words which we have borrowed from the Greek to mean what their originals meant in Plato's day. We cannot argue that, because Plato disliked democracy and advocated something approaching dictatorship, he would therefore approve of Stalin or of Mussolini and condemn representative democracy as a form of government. For, on the one hand, Greek democracy bore no resemblance to modern representative government; on the other, Plato denounced certain forms of dictatorship as tyranny. We must therefore carry our analysis far deeper than these verbal resemblances if we wish to discover what position Plato would have adopted when faced with modern problems.

To do this is not to indulge in idle speculation.

Plato was not simply a Greek who lived in the fourth century B.C. He was also (for good or for ill) the inspiration of much modern political thought and action. The *Republic* has become a part of Western European tradition: it has moulded our ways of thinking, and more than once a new interpretation of it has contributed to a great revolution which closed one epoch and inaugurated a new one. Just because the influence of Plato and Platonism has been so great, it is vital for us to-day to discover who the real Plato was and who he now is, to see him both in the Greek and in the modern world, and to appraise him as a man speaking to us and demanding our approval or our refutation. Whether we call ourselves historians or philosophers or practical men, we must treat his philosophy not merely as an historical document, but as a challenge to us, an assertion of values which we must either accept or reject. We must attempt both to recreate the historical past and to evaluate the significance of Platonism to-day: and if it is objected that this must be largely a work of imagination, it can be answered that no great historian or philosopher has ever lacked that quality.

I have decided to begin this reinterpretation with a study of democracy: it is indeed the obvious place to begin, since our modern democracy and its philosophies are rooted in Greek ideas and Greek practice. The English tradition of Locke, and even more, the French tradition of Rousseau, were consciously based on Greek models: and among practical politicians there can be few who have not gone back to Pericles for their inspiration.

This Greek tradition of popular government is still alive to-day. Men still speak with veneration of the will of the people and still claim that democracy is based upon its sovereignty. The democratic slogans are still in large part Greek slogans and it is high time that we considered what relevance they have to our practice—whether they are mere slogans or express ideals which we are trying to realize. These are precisely the questions which Plato would ask, and he would ask them in all seriousness, looking at our modern institutions, because he would see in them hardly a trace of the Greek originals which we still claim to imitate.

Let us suppose that Plato were to meet a city councillor, an ardent democrat who conscientiously occupied every leisure hour in the affairs of his borough, and was prepared to risk his life to make the world safe for democracy. Plato would be impressed by the man's sincerity and would ask him what this system was for the sake of which he was willing to sacrifice so much. The councillor would probably reply that English democracy is based on the idea of individual freedom: it is a form of government which gives to all freedom of conscience and a part in the control of the affairs of State. The Englishman detests bureaucracy and officialdom. He wishes to be ruled by plain men like himself who can interpret his wishes and make Whitehall see sense. And so we have built up our representative institutions and our political parties as instruments through which the wishes of the plain man can still be sovereign, although the executive power is largely in the hands of officials and experts. It is in this tradition of popular control that we differ from the Germans, who like being bossed and therefore accept militarism, and from the Russians, who are really not quite civilized and so put up with the autocracy and cruelty of the Bolshevik regime. We in England would not stand either of these tyrannies because we are individuals and free men who like to have a hand in running the affairs of State. We would rather muddle through in our common-sense way than surrender to theorists and cranks who claim that they know the secret of happiness and really want to impose their own ideas on everyone else.

Plato would listen politely to this speech, but he would confess at the end that he did not fully understand the references to freedom and popular control. In what sense, he would ask, are Englishmen free, and how do they control the State? He would probably be told that through elections to Parliament they choose representatives to control the bureaucracy and to decide the lines of public policy and particularly the ways in which public moneys should be spent. This answer would not satisfy him. He would point out that self-government should mean governing yourself; taking part in a general election can hardly be called that, when the actual work of government is done by a committee of members of one party in the Commons. What part, he would ask, has the people in choosing the Cabinet? It is selected by the Prime Minister from the majority party in the House, which often does not even represent the majority of the voters. So the Government may, in fact, be composed of politicians whose programme has been approved by only a minority of the nation. Plato, I fancy, would ask why we call by the name of democracy a system of government in which the people as a whole has no part, but a section of them can vote a party into power, members of which compose the actual Government. He would suggest that this scheme might well be described as "alternate party government," but he would be puzzled at the notion of calling it a government based on the will of the people.

His bewilderment would be increased when he found that in local affairs the same system is used. Here, too, the people do not govern themselves. Instead, some 30 or 40 per cent vote once a year in municipal elections. There is a little speech-making, "election addresses" are circulated, and a certain amount of canvassing is done. On the day of the election a few cars (mostly belonging to one party) can be seen, and possibly a few posters. No one seems unduly excited, and few could recognize the candidates. After this annual ceremonial the affairs of the locality are carried on very much as before.

Plato's first reaction to this discovery would be to congratulate the city councillor on the excellence of the propaganda which he and his friends employ to make the people believe that they are governing themselves when they are in fact doing nothing of the sort. His second would be one of horror when he began to realize that the councillor and others like him themselves believe that they are members of a democracy. He would conclude that they had most unmerited good fortune in having been presented by heaven with a 'noble lie' accepted by rulers and ruled alike which leaves power in the hands of the former and satisfies the vague ambitions of the latter, and he would, if he were well-disposed to us, pray that we should continue happily and for ever in our fool's paradise.

But supposing that the councillor grew irritable and said, "My dear sir, you laugh at our system: but tell me of any other in which the people really rule," Plato would reply, "That is not difficult. I will show you what your borough would look like if it were a Greek democracy. We in Greece meant by democracy the rule of the people, and we meant it literally. A Greek city of your size with, say, 100,000 inhabitants, was independent, possessed its own army and navy, and waged war upon its neighbours. I myself found such a city far too large and suggested once that 5,040 male citizens was the ideal number for a city-state. But that is by the way; if you want to introduce self-government you must first of all restrict the size of your State to at most 100,000, and it is obvious that your first requirement will be a place where all the men of the city can meet together to take all important decisions. In Athens, where the climate is dependable, we could meet out of doors, but here in England you will need a covered hall which will hold 20,000 men. For your citizen assembly will consist of all the male citizens over seventeen years of age, and it will meet at least once a month. I have suggested that you need have room for 20,000 only because I do not imagine all the 25,000 will ever come on the same day.

"This assembly will indeed be sovereign. Those citizens who trouble to attend will vote the budget after detailed discussion: will appoint by lot committees for special business, ambassadors to represent you in other towns, and generals to command your army. They will have the power to double the rates one month and to halve them the next, and they can impeach and condemn to death any unsatisfactory official. You will perhaps suggest that such an assembly is totally unmanageable. I am inclined to agree with you, but we had politicians in our best days who could command its ear for years on end, and really control city policy. They were not leaders of parties in your sense of the word, and they had no official positions. They ruled by force of personality and by the loudness of their voices, depending every day on their powers of persuasion to retain control. For the people were sovereign, and these were just ordinary citizens whom the people for the moment trusted; so that the decisions of policy were not theirs, but the people's, and they were in no sense responsible *to* the people, but only advisers *of* the people. Naturally they gained a body of support on which they could rely, and they organized political clubs and factions, but they could never gain a firm position as *rulers* because at any moment they could be voted down by the assembly. I assure you it demanded great qualities to be a politician in a city-state.

"But an assembly of 20,000 will not get through much business unless it is well prepared beforehand. So in Athens we had a preparatory council of five hundred which worked out the minutes of the assembly and drafted proposed legislation. This council also had executive powers in the intervals between meetings of the assembly, and I know you are going to interrupt me and say that in that case the people were not sovereign after all: it was the council of five hundred who really held control. In this you would be wrong: for we were democrats and took care to prevent this council ever becoming a caucus, by making membership of it depend on the *chance of the lot*. It was composed of citizens of thirty years of age and over who sat on the council for one year, and their names were pricked as you prick the names for the jury lists in England. Anyone might become a member and, as no one could be a councillor more than twice, every citizen found himself at some point in his life a member of it. And so we prevented it from ever becoming a ruling caucus since it changed from year to year and could not be packed with supporters of any politician or party.

"We believed that a democracy must be politically educated and we regarded membership of the council as the proper training for any intelligent citizen. The council had also its executive committee, membership of which went by rotation, and the chairman of the executive changed every day, so that the majority of citizens were prime minister for one day of their lives at least. My master, Socrates, once found himself on the executive on a very nasty occasion. It was after the battle of Arginusae, in 406, when we had staved off final defeat by a brilliant naval victory. The people were nervous and excitable, and when news came through that after the victory many of our boats had sunk in the storm and no efforts had been made to save the crews, a motion was introduced in the assembly to impeach all six generals and try them *en bloc*. That, of course, was illegal: each man should have had a separate trial and the chairman of the executive told the people so. But the people wanted blood and threatened to impeach him too if he threw out the motion. The executive was nervous, but Socrates said it must obey the law and face the people. He held out for a long time, but the chairman and most of the members would not risk it: so the executive gave way by a majority vote, and the generals were tried and executed *en bloc*.

"I think that will show you how much power belonged to the council, how much to the people. The people, believing in democracy, would tolerate nothing which prevented the exercise of the general will. We could have no proper civil service because it was feared that it would gain undue control: we could not even have a non-political judiciary, for the law-courts were also democratic, and nearly all cases were tried by popular juries with five hundred or one thousand members. The only important officials who were elected instead of being chosen by lot were the generals, and they could be dismissed at a moment's notice.

"You will tell me this system of government could not work. I can only reply that it continued for a very long time and that it was democratic Athens which conquered the Persians and enslaved the

Delian League, though the democracy in those days was not quite so extreme as that which I knew and have described. The system certainly worked and made every citizen who wished an active participant in the legislature and in the judiciary. But I agree that it did not work well; indeed, I denounced it heartily in every book I wrote, until I discovered that most other systems were equally bad.

"I do not imagine you are ever likely to introduce true democracy in England. For one thing your people are, as far as I can judge, profoundly un-political. They do not seem really interested in the conduct of affairs and are content if someone does that for them. They have not our feeling for collective action and collective life. If I were not your guest, I should call them unpatriotic and mercenary. They only seem to get excited about politics when their pockets are affected, and they do not really believe in themselves or their civic responsibilities. Of course, I see that no one who believes in democracy could take part in your national politics because the nation is far too big a unit to have any collective will, and the problems of national politics are too remote and difficult for the ordinary man. But if they were demo-cratic, they would be far more active in local affairs, and they would never allow you city councillors to dictate to them in the way you do. I gather that local politics in England is chiefly concerned with 'keeping down the rates,' but surely that is a very bad policy for a democracy. If your workmen were proud of your city and if they had any sense, they would see that public spending is fine, and that the poorer people can get far more benefit by it than by keeping down the rates. Instead of each trying to make his own house look well, they would build great public baths and libraries and gymnasia and gardens which everyone could enjoy: and they would see to it that a rich man who did not make large voluntary contributions as well as paying taxes was thoroughly unpopular. *The fact of the matter is that you all, rich and poor, in England behave as though you were rich.* Our rich men, of course, were anti-democratic and tried to keep the taxes down: they disliked collective life and saw that genuine culture and education is only possible for gentlemen of breeding and education. But your poor people seem to believe this as much as the rich, and to be content that they should work, while a leisured class enjoys the fruits of their labours, provided they are given enough to eat and to drink and to gamble. I regard this natural submissiveness of the English poor as the fundamental reason for the stability of your form of government: second only to that I should put the fact that, by a free use of the wealth which your empire and your mineral resources have provided, you have been able to tame the natural leaders of democracy and to give them bribes enough to take the sting out of their speeches and the revolutionary spirit out of their grumbles and their discontent.

"Your country is, in fact, a lucky blend of aristocracy and oligarchy whose social structure is rendered stable by the 'noble lie' of self-government and individual freedom. By retaining the loyal services of a gentry schooled to political responsibility, you have avoided the open class-war which plutocracy inevitably brings. By allowing your industrialists and merchants to grow fabulously rich, you have made them contented and patriotic citizens, and have then skilfully removed their sons from their mercenary influence and trained them in boarding schools and universities in the ideals of your aristocracy. Thus their highest wish is not to be rich only, but to gain a title as well, and their desire for aristocratic status softens the acquisitive instinct and moulds it into the service of the community.

"I myself have little respect for this British ideal of *titled wealth*, but I must confess that, once the end is admitted, the means you have taken to achieve it are wholly correct; and since you and your countrymen have no feeling for philosophy or metaphysics, I shall assume in talking to you that your ideals are sound. Of course they are not, but they are less vicious than those of most nations which I have visited.

"Admitting then for the moment the correctness of the end, I regard your form of government as very skilfully adapted to achieve it. Your social system has remained rooted in *status*, not in equality, and you have therefore achieved in England something not unlike the class-divisions which I tried to work out in my *Republic*. Each 'civilian'[1] tries to retain his position as craftsman or doctor or lawyer or shopkeeper: he is content with that because he regards the established order as ordained by God, and therefore limits his ambitions to securing his place within

---

[1] See page 121.

that order. The few who are naturally ambitious may wish to climb a step higher on the social ladder, but they do not wish to knock the ladder down, and for this reason the ambitious are, more than all others, upholders of the inequality which is the essence of that order. They believe in my idea of justice 'that each man should do his own proper business, and that only the best should rule.'

"I am especially interested to see how this notion of status has captured the workmen among whom I should have expected the ideas of democracy to thrive. Instead of uniting to overthrow the rich, they have set up combinations and unions to defend their status, and these unions compete with one another as much as they struggle against the employers. Craft is matched against craft, skilled against unskilled, and finally the employed feel themselves bound together against those social outcasts, the unemployed. For the unemployed have lost status and are therefore the care of no union or combination of workmen at all. Then, again, I notice among the workmen that division of ruler and subject which I was at such pains to impose on the city-state. There, too, you find a hierarchy with officials and politicians at the top, and below, the subject masses, who even in union and party matters do not wish to rule themselves but are content to leave that task to others whom they trust and who, because of their high rank, are well content to leave the world as it is, instead of turning it upside down.

"In assessing the goodness and badness of any social system or state, you will agree that the details of political organization are relatively unimportant and are always secondary to social habits and tradition. Your tradition is, if I understand it, an aristocratic tradition which has maintained itself through unprecedented economic changes. Your aristocrats have conformed themselves to the dominance of large-scale manufacture more skilfully than ours faced the growth of trade and commerce. Without serious disturbance they have habituated the new industrial leaders to their old traditions, so that the whole population retains its old loyalties and status in a new setting. They prefer good government to self-government, and they have only demanded the extension of privilege where it could be granted without any danger. Whenever a section has pressed its claims too far, the people has rallied to the Government, assuming that justice is always on the side of law and order, and that any claim of justice is unreasonable if it involves any risk for those who are pretty well content with their lot.

"I have been told of the General Strike which occurred in 1926, and I have been deeply impressed by the movement of public opinion on that occasion. To begin with it was favourable to the miners, but immediately the situation threatened to upset the wages and salaries of the 'civilians,' not only the public, who were unaffected by the immediate issue, but the workmen's leaders and many of the workmen themselves became hesitant in their pressure and the strike collapsed, with the result that the miners were worse off than before. Again, I am told that the English people has the cause of the unemployed at heart, but in 1931 it voted into power (and I believe many of the unemployed were in agreement) a Government resolved to reduce the payments made to them. These two examples demonstrate to my mind a social tradition of unheard of strength, which is able to stifle the cries of the suffering and outcast by the mere suggestion that if they are listened to and if their woes are remedied, the status of the other 'civilians' will be in serious danger of attack.

"It is therefore clear that you have the good fortune to be possessed of a temper which shrinks before all thought of poverty, and therefore condemns all changes which may endanger the national income, and which prefers the preservation of status to the amelioration of suffering or the claims of justice. And I fancy that the political system which you call representative government is the expression of this temper. First of all, in the monarchy and in the House of Lords, you have preserved institutions whose only purpose is to delay changes and prevent hurried legislation. Secondly, in your House of Commons, with its first, second, and third readings and all its other ceremonial of discussion and debate, you have evolved a legislature which must listen to every minority and vested interest and make concessions to them. By this means all violent legislation is robbed of its sting and rendered relatively impotent. For an injured minority is always more vociferous and persuasive than the great mass of the people who will be benefited by reform. Thus in the interest of the landowner and the speculator your legislature has resolutely refused to protect the countryside from chaotic and ugly building, or your new roads from being rendered useless by the erection of houses along their whole length. I believe that your legislature, since its ideal is not justice or beauty but titled wealth, has been wise in its decision to sacrifice beauty and the health of the people on this issue. For once property is challenged, a spirit is aroused in the masses most difficult to control. I could quote you many other examples of the same wisdom. You have allowed your transport and your coal mining, for instance, to become involved in unfortunate difficulties, but wisely refused to give way to a democratic demand that the people should own them, because you well realize that a docile people and chaotic industry are preferable to that ugly greed and self-assertiveness which always grow up when the people begin to speak with one mind against its natural rulers, and to show a preference for justice against the claims of salary and status. You are, in fact, convinced that the maintenance of an ancestral social tradition is worth the suffering of many, and that that suffering would be increased were their claims to be heard.

"It is an especial virtue, however, of your political organization that the criticisms and wishes of the people are not entirely disregarded but caught up and satisfied in the 'noble lie' of representative institutions. By your system of changing governments you do—it is true—concede some slight influence to the popular will. In so doing you run the very greatest of perils. But how ingeniously you canalize it into the mere choice between two or three political parties, so that the people shall not choose their representatives but only choose between the candidates dictated to them by those who control the party machines: how skilfully you prevent any but these traditional parties from growing up and any but a tiny minority of wealthy persons or lawyers or trade-union officials from standing for Parliament! Thus the people are never represented by men or women like themselves but by professional politicians well versed in the rules of the game, and prepared to defend it against all change. And if by any chance some simple man or crazy idealist is elected, how soon he is charmed and beguiled by the ceremonial and, far off from the miseries he is resolved to cure, how rapidly he ceases to be the spokesman of the people, and becomes a Member of Parliament proud of his status and stalwart for its tradition.

"And so you have taught the people to talk in an educated tone through their representatives, and persuaded them to prefer the parliamentary tradition to true democracy. You have taken that great monster the popular will and divided it into a myriad parts, each speaking for itself, and each interested only in its own salvation, and you have given them spokesmen who will attune their demands to the maintenance of the established order.

"You should indeed be well satisfied. And yet I am told that there are among you malcontents and agitators who look with longing at our Athenian system and wish to increase the influence of the people on your affairs. Be well advised and suppress such people at once. Their hearts are better than their heads; and good intentions in politics are more dangerous than cool villainy. Consider the little that the people do now. Do they do it well? Can they correct the expert's opinion on scales of relief for the unemployed or peace terms for the Abyssinians? They cannot, because they do not know the facts and have not been trained to give judgment upon them. For this reason, when dealing with questions remote from their daily life, they will take decisions flowing out of sentiment instead of based firmly on cool thought, and will surrender, in a watery feeling of unselfishness, interests and power which they can ill afford to lose. The truth is that the people need good government, but that cannot mean popular government in either sense of the word 'popular.' For popular government must mean weak government and short-sighted government: weak because it does not risk the anger of the people even for its own good; short-sighted, because the people cannot see beyond the ends of their noses.

"But there is a second danger in popular control which is even more serious. If you look at politics you will find that most people's interest is in their own pockets. The rich want the Government to protect the wealth they have amassed; the poor want the Government, by taxation and social services, to redistribute the wealth of the rich. What will happen then if you allow the democratic control of the machine of government? Obviously the rich will want to use it to favour their business, and to protect their property: they will only use the social services as a sop to keep the masses quiet. But the poor will want to use it for squeezing all they can out of the rich and distributing the benefits among themselves. And so popular control of government must degenerate into anarchy: polite party politics will disappear: class-war will take its place. The freedom which the democrat claims will be a freedom of the *two nations*, the rich and the poor, to fight it out between themselves who shall have the larger slice of the cake. And what will happen to the politician? He will not be able to rule for the good of the nation, because if he tries to do that he will never get to power. Only a man willing to defend the interests of either the rich or the poor will be a success. Anyone who is fairminded and really wants justice will be shoved aside by the two great factions: and so your politician will merely become a skilled orator, whose job it is to put his client's case without any regard for justice or principles.

"But everyone will talk about justice and right and honour and integrity and so on. The words and phrases will go on being used by both sides in order to win the support of the masses. For both sides need propaganda, and the best propaganda for a bad cause is high-sounding moral principles. But in spite of the speeches of the politicians, a really democratic nation, in which there are great inequalities of wealth, must be a nation divided against itself: an uneasy equilibrium of contending forces which may at any moment turn into the dictatorship of the rich or the dictatorship of the poor. Only so long as there is money enough to satisfy the demands of the poor can it survive. When wealth runs short one or other of the two gangs will seize control, for real democracy means anarchy and class-war. You should thank the Providence which has protected you from it and made you content to dilute authority with freedom. The seeds of conflict between rich and poor are there to-day. They will grow monstrously if you water them with real popular control.

"That you should do anything of the sort, my dear sir, is in the highest degree improbable; and I recognize that warnings of this kind are totally unnecessary in England. For the safest defence against real democracy is the 'noble lie' of Representative Government such as you possess. With us democracy was a revolutionary and subversive force: with you it is the greatest single influence on the side of law and order. By adopting it your rich men have preserved their riches, your gentry their professions, and your working classes have persuaded themselves that they too are rich. You are the most complacent and therefore the most conservative country in the world. Unless by some mischance you lose your empire, or by some divine intervention become philosophical, nothing can shake your self-content."

I have imagined Plato discussing England with a moderately intelligent supporter of the *status quo* who believed that he was a democrat. The reader may feel that he has not grappled with the problem seriously, and I believe that in fact he would refuse to do so unless his opponent were willing to dip below the surface, to forget legal fictions and constitutional forms and discover the real basis of our social system. This the ordinary democrat refuses to do: he talks cheerfully of the sovereignty of the people, the power of public opinion, individual freedom, and civil liberty, and he preaches that these are the real values of our English system which we must be prepared to defend against all comers. Plato would attempt to show him that these are only trimmings: the real basis of our social tradition is totally different. What we need to-day is not more popular control or more education, but a clear understanding by the ruling classes of their responsibilities and of the dangers which face the country, and to this end he would probably propose that we should consider the problem of education next.

6 PLATO LOOKS AT BRITISH EDUCATION

PLATO I am told that you Englishmen, realizing that the proper upbringing of children is the most important factor in affairs of State, and that a happy community can never be achieved unless the education be good, have decided to grapple seriously with the problem and base your education in future upon sound principles.

EDUCATIONALIST Yes, we have. And we have made some very real advances during the last fifty years. You probably do not realize that in 1870 we had no State system of education at all. Parents were not compelled to send their children to school; there were no Public Schools for girls, and very few good ones for boys. A Nonconformist was practically debarred from higher education at school or university, however rich he was, and for the poor it was wellnigh impossible, even in cases of real ability, to obtain any sound education at all. But that has all been changed. We have compulsory education for all up to the age of fourteen (it would be fifteen but for the cowardice of the Government): we have secondary education in day-schools up to eighteen for at least a good percentage of those who deserve it, and we have a number of universities which, with the aid of State moneys, carry on higher education up to the age of twenty-two or twenty-three.

PLATO You have certainly not been inactive, and I congratulate you on refusing to entrust to the family or other irresponsible private persons the education of the coming generation. But I am not quite clear about one or two points. To begin with, why have you concentrated your energies on providing education for all and sundry?

EDUCATIONALIST   One of the reasons is undoubtedly our belief in justice. We are democrats and we think that education should not be the perquisite of one class but should be open to all. It is no use giving a man a vote unless he can use it, and universal education is the only way of making universal suffrage a reality and not a sham. You can have representative government and parliament and all the institutions of democracy, even the voting at elections, but they will all be mere shams unless you have universal education too. Institutions cannot make a country democratic unless the people have the knowledge and capacity to use them. That knowledge and that capacity do not drop out of heaven. It costs money and energy to create them, and we are trying to do that in England through our school system. We do not want only to polish and scrape our children into neat little cogs which fit precisely into the State machine and spend their lives mechanically revolving with perfect precision, to be pensioned off when they are worn out. In fact, we do not want our children only to be good technicians, we want them to be citizens of a democracy as well; competent to play their part in their trade union or the committee of their football club, or their city council or even in Parliament. We want to teach them to rule themselves and to help to rule the country. And so we do not only teach "the subjects which pay" in our schools, and we do not only train the children for jobs. We teach them history and geography and economics, and we try to make them able to give a sensible judgment about politics.

PLATO All that you say agrees with something I read in a speech of one of your statesmen, that universal education is an experiment in self-government. I was interested in that remark because I myself have some experience of a State where all the citizens took a hand in government. I did not consider the experiment a success, and I should like to know what the results of your venture here may be. Do the people now demand a revolution in England and wish to take control of affairs?

EDUCATIONALIST Yes, I think they do. You can see the results particularly in foreign policy. Before the war that was something in which the masses took no interest. Now, through the efforts of the school teachers and the League of Nations Union, public interest in foreign affairs has been aroused. At question time in the House, the Foreign Minister is bombarded with questions, deputations are constantly sent to him and to the Prime Minister, and in every home in England the issues of peace and war are strenuously discussed.

PLATO And has this improved the foreign policy of your country?

EDUCATIONALIST It has certainly made it impossible for any Government to carry on the secret diplomacy and power politics of the bad old days. The Peace Ballot was an event of real international importance, and one of its direct results was the repudiation of the Hoare–Laval proposals. The Foreign Minister was compelled to resign on that occasion by the sheer force of public opinion.

PLATO   But he has returned to the Ministry, has he not? And the Abyssinians have been conquered? I did not doubt that universal education *had* influenced foreign policy. My question was whether you believed that it had influenced it for the good.

EDUCATIONALIST   It has given the Government a new sense of its responsibility to the electorate. It can no longer do just what it wants.

PLATO   But suppose it wants to do something sensible which the public refuses to accept?

EDUCATIONALIST   We believe that it is better that the people should do something foolish, if they have really made up their minds, than that they should be *forced* to do what is right against their will.

PLATO   Then you believe that freedom is better than virtue?

EDUCATIONALIST   No, I don't. I believe virtue is impossible without freedom. You cannot compel a child to be good—far less a grown man or woman.

PLATO   Perhaps you are right. But then why do you have any government at all? If you wish your countrymen to learn by the bitter experience of their own mistakes and to do what they like provided they do it with a will, isn't it better to abolish the State altogether?

EDUCATIONALIST   You are just twisting my remarks so that they sound like nonsense. Of course you must stop people acting in ways which disturb the freedom of others: that is the purpose of the State.

But, as far as possible, you must leave them free to make all important decisions for themselves. Our purpose as educationalists to-day is to train up an electorate capable of understanding the issues on which they are called to vote, not experts on economics and politics, but men and women imbued with sound political judgment. . . .

PLATO But you admit that you haven't done that yet. And still, before your educational reforms are finished, you wish to entrust a half-educated electorate with intricate political decisions. Surely that is putting the cart before the horse. First you should have a system of universal education which produces citizens of the type you describe, and then perhaps you could safely entrust them with the control of policy. But surely, when you have achieved a perfectly educated electorate you will not need a government at all.

EDUCATIONALIST You are back again on the same point. Of course, the world is not ideal and never will be. You have to take it as you find it, and we believe that by entrusting ordinary people with the control of their destinies you are giving them that freedom without which all talk of virtue and morality is absurd.

PLATO But you said just now that the purpose of the State was to prevent men encroaching on the rights of others, to compel them against their will to do their own jobs and leave their neighbours alone. If that is so, then surely the State must, in its foreign policy too, prevent its citizens encroaching on the rights of others. And yet you wish your citizens to instruct the Government in its conduct of international affairs. Will this not mean that the foreign policy of England in the future will be actuated by the self-interest and greed of Englishmen anxious to maintain and extend their empire, and to increase their well-being at the cost of others?

EDUCATIONALIST We expect the exact opposite. It is not the people who want wars and empires, but the armament manufacturers and the capitalists. The people want peace and international justice.

PLATO Well, that is a very splendid thing. But do they know how to realize their ideals? I can tell you from personal experience that diplomacy is a very fine art and that military and naval science cannot be learnt in a day. Are the people experienced in the technique of politics and versed in the history of international relations? or are they just full of noble sentiments which, coming into contact with reality, explode like a bubble on a rock?

EDUCATIONALIST We try to teach them all that, but we believe that what our world really needs is a little less cunning and a good deal more simple straight-forward morality.

PLATO I agree: sound moral sentiments are all that is necessary for a 'civilian' or even for an 'administrator.'[1] But they are not sufficient for a ruler, and your people are to become rulers in your experiment in self-government. For that they will need a great deal more. Statesmanship is a highly skilled profession and you must distinguish the sort of education which a statesman needs from that of a 'civilian.' He must know both the principles of his policy, and the

[1] See page 121.

world in which the policy is to be realized. In this particular he is like any other craftsman. A man may have a great appreciation of pictures and be full of admirable aesthetic emotions: but that would not be enough to qualify him as a painter. To be a painter he needs a knowledge of the principles of painting and of the materials, the mixing of colours, the canvas, the brushes, and so on—and a bit of inspiration besides. The same is true of ruling. The ruler must not only have the right moral feelings such as a belief in justice and peace, he must also know the principles of his craft and understand the everyday world of politics in which he is to practise it. But with regard to foreign affairs, it is by no means easy to attain the necessary experience or knowledge of the facts, simply because it is the essence of diplomacy that if negotiations are to be successful they must be secret until they are completed. So I do not understand how all citizens are to become qualified to criticize and alter the policy of your Government.

EDUCATIONALIST They cannot, of course, control the details of day to day policy: but they should decide the main lines which the policy should follow.

PLATO I disagree. For the main lines are all important and it needs a philosopher to solve the problems of peace and war, of imperialism and defence. But let us leave foreign policy and return to your educational reforms. You stated that your ideal was universal education for all, and I imagine you will soon mention "an equal chance for all." Why exactly do you wish to achieve this end?

EDUCATIONALIST It is only common justice that every child should have an equal chance.

PLATO A chance of what?

EDUCATIONALIST A chance of realizing its innate capacities to the full and of attaining a university education.

PLATO Clearly that is so. You wish rightly to allot to each child the vocation in life which suits it best and to limit entrance to the university only to those who can profit by it.

EDUCATIONALIST Yes, that is our aim, and with this in view, we have built up an educational pyramid, with elementary schools as the base, secondary schools in the middle, and the university as the apex.

PLATO And would you regard anyone as fully educated who had not taken a university degree?

EDUCATIONALIST No, I should not.

PLATO Then why in heaven's name do you allow him to vote and to control the destinies of the State when you yourself admit that he is incapable of doing so? For if the vast majority of children are not worthy to pass beyond the school, and only a tiny minority are fit to profit by study in the university, then, surely, we have almost completed our demonstration that the people should be relieved of a responsibility they cannot bear, and that political power should be entrusted only to the man or woman who has passed with distinction the examinations which the universities impose.

EDUCATIONALIST That is all very well in theory, but we do not believe in England that academic education is the only qualification for political responsibilities. Indeed, we find that most of our university professors show small political sense compared to those who have been schooled in the university of life.

PLATO But if you really believe that, why have you introduced university education at all? Why not leave it to providence or life (call it what you like) to produce your rulers? It served you well in the past, and it may (for all that you or I know) continue to serve you in the future. If you do not believe that education has the power to train a man and to fit him better for his job, whether it be banking or carpentering, or ruling the State, then I would advise you to give up your brave experiment altogether and to trust to your English god called "muddle through."

EDUCATIONALIST It is quite impossible to discuss education with a man who sacrifices everything to logical consistency. Our system in England cannot be logical because it has developed out of an historical past. It is full of inconsistencies and ambiguities precisely because it is not imposed by educational tyrants but fitted into a complex historical tradition.

PLATO That may well be—and yet in forming your educational policy and in deciding the direction in which your social tradition should move, you must have principles of action, and it is these which I am trying to elucidate in the course of our conversation. Consistency and logic are not, after all, positive defects even in an Englishman!

I believe that your inability to answer my simple questions indicates a real uncertainty in your mind about the aims you have in view. You have not yet made up your mind what education is for: and yet you are busy opening new schools and agitating for the raising of the school-leaving age. Let me put the matter to you quite clearly. There is such a thing as technical education, is there not? And we mean by it the training of a person for a special vocation or job?

EDUCATIONALIST Yes.

PLATO Now it is possible to believe that all education should be technical, since every man has a job to which he is by nature fitted, and to which he can be trained. The farmer can be taught farming, the builder building, and so on. And since you yourself have admitted that there is such a job as ruling, then must there not be a special sort of education which will enable a man to practise the art of government really well? Is that so?

EDUCATIONALIST Perhaps.

PLATO I shall assume that "perhaps" in this case implies the reluctant agreement of reason hampered by prejudice. Since you agree therefore that there is or there could be a special training for rulers, let us now consider if your present university education is a training of this sort. What do you think?

EDUCATIONALIST Well, as it is largely based on the ideas you put forward in the *Republic*, I presume that you expect the answer "yes."

PLATO I was certainly pleased to discover that in your universities research is combined with general education, and to observe that abstract theory is regarded as essential to sound education. But I am not so well pleased by your suggestion that in

England university graduates are considered unsuitable for statesmanship. I expect the reason is that most of the young men who attend your universities are concerned, not to prepare themselves for politics, but to gain a special craft-training, which will enable them to earn their living in industry or commerce or the civil service. If this is the case, then your universities no longer preserve the ideals of my Academy, but are becoming technical high schools for the production of skilled craftsmen who must remain for ever remote from politics, technicians with their interest in the mill or the office and not in the supreme affairs of State.

EDUCATIONALIST Perhaps they are. We certainly do not regard our universities as mere schools for politicians, or exclude from them men and women with special aptitudes for research, or even those who merely wish for a general education. We want to give each a chance to develop in his own way, not to dragoon them all into politics.

PLATO I presume from what you say that you are satisfied with your present politicians: otherwise you could not afford to let each child follow its own bent so that often the very best of them, for the sake of personal interests, deny all the responsibilities which superior intelligence imposes upon them, and employ themselves on activities which contribute nothing or very little to the common good.

EDUCATIONALIST I think you have an inflated idea of the importance of the politician. A country is not really run by politicians but by the civil servants, and those in responsible positions in industry and commerce. They are the really important people: the politicians are mostly tub-thumpers and don't get very much done.

PLATO But now I am really confused. You do not by any chance elect your civil servants or your technicians or industrial administrators, do you?

EDUCATIONALIST No, of course not.

PLATO And yet you tell me that in your democracy they are the really important people and the politicians are merely talkers. But if this is so, how can your people claim to have political freedom and to control their rulers? Really I don't understand you at all. You would seem to suggest that your democratic institutions are only a sham, a gaily painted hoarding, behind which you keep hidden the Government and the machinery of State. I believe you are right in this, and that your educational system is not intended to promote general education such as will equip all to be *rulers*, but to produce men and women each skilled in his or her job and each filled with a noble sentiment of public service. But if this is so, please admit it openly and contradict all those former statements you made about universal education being an experiment in self-government. For it is clear that if you believe that education should train children to their proper vocations, then you must admit that as those vocations vary, so the education will vary too.

EDUCATIONALIST Yes, we believe that.

PLATO And you will be compelled to make a distinction between the education suitable for those in highly responsible positions and for those who are merely engaged in some mechanical or craft labour, admitting that to the former belong higher education, while the latter need only a technical proficiency in their trades.

EDUCATIONALIST I am not so sure. We believe that everyone should be given something more than a merely vocational training. For they all are human beings with latent possibilities of culture and reasoning: and so all must be given a general education as well.

PLATO But do you give the same general education to the less gifted and to the more gifted alike?

EDUCATIONALIST No, that is impossible. For one thing the majority stop going to school at the age of fourteen; and for another, they would not all appreciate a university syllabus.

PLATO How profoundly I agree! The lower orders, those whom I called "civilians" in my State, do not for the most part appreciate philosophy, and the few who do are taken in by the first impostor whom they meet, a pseudo-philosopher or a popular scientist with a clever turn of phrase and a cheap theology. Popular taste is always vulgar and can in no way discriminate between a cheap imitation and the truth. That is why I suggested that the masses should be forbidden access to true knowledge and be fed on myths and fairy stories and religious ceremonials—"noble lies" I called them—which the Government should concoct to satisfy their craving for enlightenment and for a solution of those ultimate questions which they idly discuss in their spare time. I have heard that a neighbour State to yours has built up a Ministry of Propaganda and Popular

Enlightenment, and I am delighted with the idea. It suggests that there, at least, there are statesmen who appreciate the dangers of uncontrolled enlightenment and literature and music and see that such things may pervert the minds of the less intelligent and excite them to serious disorders and unrest.

EDUCATIONALIST I believe you are no better than a Fascist. How can you approve of propaganda and the enslavement of public opinion to the lies and half-truths of the Nazi politicians? It means the destruction of all freedom.

PLATO But are your people really free? Are they not also enslaved to lies and half-truths which are pumped into them daily by the newspapers and the cinemas and the novelists and the preachers and even by your League of Nations Union?

EDUCATIONALIST Of course I dislike the penny press and the dreadful stuff which the cinema producers put out. But at least an Englishmen is free to *choose*: he does not have to listen to one monotonous stream of propaganda, but can hear all sides of the case and form his own judgment.

PLATO Please do not go so quickly. You say he is free to choose and select, but how can he do that if he has no criterion by which to choose and select and so discover the truth? He cannot: and so he stands dazed and bewildered by an astonishing variety of nonsensical fantasies which buzz in his ears and jumble themselves together until he does not know whether he is standing on his head or his feet. I admit that it may be more amusing to listen to many untruths rather than to a single one, but I do not understand why you claim that a man is free in the former case and a slave in the latter. The fact is that if he cannot distinguish truth from falsehood he is never free, whether he lives in England or in Germany or in Athens.

And so, when I seriously consider your great experiment in self-government, I perceive that it is no such thing. For the general education you so highly praise does not make the masses free, but inculcates only a false self-esteem and pretentiousness, with the result that they are not less but more liable to be misled and deceived by the rogues and tricksters whose profession it is to sell Enlightenment and Culture to them. It is not the humble craftsman but the half-educated upon whom the advertiser and the quack and the get-rich-quick merchants thrive. The proof of this is simple. If your general education were really successful, it would drive out the advertiser altogether and compel the quack to migrate to another land. But that has not happened in your country. Instead, the more "educated" your people become, the more easily they are swindled and deceived by the self-same trickery, decked out in the trappings of science and culture and even of religion.

And the same is true of politics. There, too, your general education will not enable the common people to think for themselves: it will only make them falsely believe that they can do so, and so make them more susceptible to the arts of propaganda and advertisement. Each man being skilled in his own job and being provided with a little general education besides, will hold himself competent to judge of matters where he has no experience or knowledge. How easy it will be then for an orator who has money enough in his pocket and insolence in his heart, to propose some high-sounding scheme and to enslave his countrymen to himself with a new myth which both satisfies their bestial emotions and tickles their educational pretensions. I have been told of strange sophistries named Buchmannism and Social Credit and Christian Science which thrive in your country: and I believe that you will not be able to deny that it is the "educated" among your citizens who chiefly support them with their money and devotion. Such foolishness is in itself unimportant, but it should be a warning to you that human nature is tougher and less manageable than you educators believe. Man demands not truth but wonders and miracles, and will, if he is given the opportunity, enslave himself to any superstition rather than accept the commands of knowledge. For truth is seldom comforting, and reality has rarely the winning aspect with which deception can deck itself out.

It is for this reason that you should now take warning if you are really concerned for the happiness and virtue of your countrymen. For you have infected them with false standards and made them believe that knowledge is easy to come by and open to everyone who has read a book or heard a lecture. And so your democracy, which you praise as the home of freedom and the protector of the conscience of the individual, is in reality not far removed from the dictatorships you abhor. In the latter the people are enslaved to a single lie: in the former to many, and freedom belongs neither to the purveyors of untruth, nor to its luckless purchasers. For even your film magnates and your newspaper kings, your makers of cosmetics and salves, your political bosses and your orators and publicists, are not free to do what they please: they too are enslaved since, to keep their circulations up and their tills full, they must dance attendance on a stupid public, ministering to its every whim and considering only what new sensation they can provide to titillate its jaded palate.

The free spirit indeed brought up in such an exotic luxuriance of trickery and deceit will have only one refuge. He will not believe one word which is told him by the politician or the publicist or the advertiser or anyone else, but keep himself to himself until such a time as truth can gain control and rule your country.

EDUCATIONALIST I suspected that you were a Fascist from the first and now I am sure of it. You have no respect for your fellow-men, and very little kindness or love in your nature. You want to boss everybody and make them believe what you believe. Well, you won't ever be popular in this country, I can assure you.

PLATO That is possible, but I at least am not willing to conceal the truth even for the sake of winning favour among your countrymen. And yet I am not so sure that they will detest me: for they have more sense in their heads than you believe, and until, quite recently, men of your sentiments attained power, they possessed a very sensible educational system.

EDUCATIONALIST So you want us to go back to the days of public ignorance and public schools.

PLATO No, I do not wish you to go backwards, for

that is impossible; but I would remind you that the old is not necessarily bad, nor the new good. In the old days, before your universal education and democracy, your country was not ashamed to be divided into two classes, the gentry and the common people. The latter were craftsmen and mechanics and farmers, who delighted in their work and were proficient at it. With no general education, they led happy and contented lives, trusting their superiors to manage the affairs of State, and believing the stories which the Churches told them about virtue and sin and the future life. I must remind you that it was in those days that England won her empire and produced the artists and men of letters for whom she is justly famed. The rulers then were men of substance aware of their responsibilities and firm in the knowledge that an aristocracy and a Church are necessary to any stable society.

You mentioned the public schools just now, and I must say that from what I hear of them, they must have been at one time excellent institutions. They removed the boys of the ruling class from the influence of their parents and gave them a sound training in morals and literature and gymnastics, without any pretensions to "intellectual" training. And so they engraved on their souls an ideal of obedience and loyalty to tradition which made them in good time sound administrators and soldiers, resolute to conserve the constitution of the country and to defend it against all change. Cut off from the mollycoddling and sentiment which mothers will always heap on their children, remote from the petty cares of money and poverty, living in beautiful buildings and licking each other into shape as boys only can, they grew up to be true gentlemen, devoted servants of the established order, and as judges or civil servants or administrators, to preserve a noble tradition of impartiality and justice.

These things I consider to be good and worthy of preservation, and I would advise you (if I didn't know that persuasion with men of your unreasoning nature is useless) to enshrine them in your new educational system. But I do not believe them perfect for three very good reasons. In the first place, those who had learnt these ideals at their schools were not set under the control of philosophers, but of men no better than themselves who, having no real understanding of the eternal principles which govern human affairs, were not able to keep in check and to control the technicians and merchants and industrialists. And so, as time went on and inventions were made which gave to your country vast wealth at no very great cost of labour or thought, your administration gradually allowed the motives of greed and power to overwhelm those of reason and self-control, until desire for profit ruled your State, and without your administrators or your priests ever suspecting such a thing, they became the slaves of imperialism instead of the servants of reason. I admit that their natural good qualities softened this imperialism and often annulled its worst effects, but I would warn you that until the ownership of property in land or currency is forbidden to your rulers, and until they are wise and powerful enough to arrest

the profit motive and to imprison it, you cannot rest
secure of your country's prosperity.

In the second place, your public schools have
always been private institutions uncontrolled by the
State and open only to those who had money enough
and to spare. Perhaps this was no bad thing when the
State was controlled by merchants and bankers and
suchlike people, but in a just society they would be
in the hands of the rulers and open to all who could
profit by them. In the third place, your universities
have never fully recognized the task which God had
in store for them. They have permitted the State to
be seduced by the profit motive and enchained to
the machine of money-making, and so the natural
rulers who frequent them can no longer guide the
machine, but have become servants of it.

From all that I have said, you will see what reforms
I would suggest. You must begin at the top and
rebuild your universities and imbue them with the
desire to provide for your country rulers worthy of
it. I do not pretend that this will be easy to do. Learned
men, though they often mention me with praise,
have so little understood the spirit of my Academy
that they have actually perverted the word "academic"
so that it now means something remote from practical
life. I can well understand their hatred and contempt
for the world outside, and their unwillingness to
admit that they themselves have renounced it only
because they were unable to impress the men of
action, who control affairs, with their superior learning. But you will agree that unless they regain the
belief that the reason they serve can and must rule

the world, they will be of little use to their country-men or to the world.

This is most unlikely to happen: for professors who lead a comfortable life and combine personal security with a conviction of their own righteousness are seldom prepared to risk these things in the attempt to help others. Your universities therefore will probably remain content to be servants not critics of the world they live in, salving their consciences by the pro-motion of a little useless learning and by lip-service to the ideals of academic freedom and impartiality.

In this case you must (as I did) set up a rival to all existing institutions, resolved to serve only the cause of truth, and to proclaim that truth to all. You will be accused of bias and of subversive teaching and of destroying the ideals of academic sobriety. But you will not listen to these taunts because you know that the academic who is not also a man of action is no true son of the academy. In your new university you will once again combine scientific research with a training for statesmanship, and you will set up over its portals the motto, "Knowledge alone shall rule." Strong in this belief, you will welcome all accusations of partiality and of subversive teaching, knowing well that a new truth is always the exposure of false-hood and that impartiality is usually the cloak for a tame submission to the established order. And there is one other change you must make in the beliefs of your young men. At present they are gentle-hearted and inspired with the naïve belief that truth and wisdom can prevail by their natural virtue against force and cunning. And so they go forth unarmed to conquer the world and soon come home with a bruise on their heads and disillusionment in their hearts, having discovered that wickedness, which delights in violence, is an enemy who cannot be softened with smooth words and noble sentiments, but must be beaten down and bound fast with fetters of steel so that it shall not raise its head again. This lesson you must teach daily in your new university, and set up as a second motto over its doors, "No pacifist shall enter here": and you must constantly remind your pupils, since in the history of mankind the rule of reason has never once been established by kindness or speeches only, that the philosopher must be prepared to use force and violence not less but more resolutely than his opponents. For his cause will always be more unpopular than the half-truths and easy salves with which his enemies beguile the people, and therefore must be enforced with every rigour and austerity, until the ignoble passions of the masses have become tamed and subdued to the rule of knowledge. Let your young men therefore know well that if they desire to save their country from destruction, they must not only be inspired by the peaceful spirit of research, but schooled in the discipline of military science, which shrinks from no bloodshed for the sake of the common good.

When your new university is firmly established and has begun to gain control of the affairs of State, you must next turn your attention to the schools. Here you must not be perturbed by the bogeys of Fascism and National Socialism, which you just now mentioned, but must be willing to admit that even a bad Government may have good ideas, and that it is the duty of the statesman to examine without bias or prejudice the institutions of other lands. So you will be pleased and confirmed in your traditions when you see that the Germans and the Italians have aped your national customs, introducing and refining your public school system to suit the modern world, and you will therefore cling fast to this system and make it the centre of your future schooling. You will take over the existing schools and will openly proclaim that they are to be the breeding ground of your political leaders, segregating carefully the children who are best fitted for this responsibility from those who will be contented with a civilian life. For the latter you will provide technical schools where they can learn the craft to which they are best suited, and because this class is of small importance to the State, you will leave them with their parents and only compel them to attend the schools by day. But for the former you will prepare a sterner education and you will forbid them to visit their homes except on feast days and public holidays. Beginning with the existing schools, you will compel them to return to the Spartan simplicity of earlier days. You will dismiss their nurses and matrons and the pseudo-fathers and mothers who by their kindness and soft sentiments destroy the tough fibre of their youth. In these schools too you will put boys and girls together and make no distinction between them, remembering always that your task is to bring up a race of soldiers and administrators, not of elegantly cultured ladies and gentlemen such as are now produced by the

M

schools. And so the discipline must be harsh, and mind and body alike must be trained to accuracy and obedience and efficiency, and to the appreciation of an austere and simple beauty such as would not shame a soldier. For this reason you will teach them the elements of mathematics and science and the study of language, and will combine with these the learning of the noblest of your national literature and music, and a soldierly type of sport and gymnastic.

When you have done all this, you will find it an easy task to solve the problem of general education for the masses which we were discussing just now. Realizing that they are incompetent to rule themselves, you will seek above all to induce in them a spirit of loyal submissiveness to the rulers: and since you cannot restore the influence of your Church, which fulfilled this task in the past, you must suppress those warring religious sects altogether, and invent a new political religion, punishing by death any citizen who dares to preach a doctrine other than yours. This you can only do if you are masters of the printing press, the wireless, and all your modern methods of communication, and you will therefore make a second law forbidding the unlicensed sale of opinions and superstitions (whether written or spoken or sung) on pain of death. Then when you have done all this, you can allow what general education you please, provided that you are clear in your own mind that such education or popular enlightenment (call it what you will) is not knowledge or science at all, but "a noble lie" suited to the intelligence of those who can never attain true wisdom or knowledge of God.

EDUCATIONALIST Thank you very much indeed for your suggestions. I am sure they would be most acceptable to Sir Oswald Mosley.

PLATO I do not know the gentleman, but if they are acceptable to him, then he has been sadly misrepresented to me by those who do.

IN the two previous chapters we have seen something of the modern Plato's attitude to British democracy, and of his suggestions for its reform. Not content to examine institutions or modes of government, he has tried to analyse the social tradition which inspires them and to discover the principles according to which its development should proceed. His advice can be summed up quite briefly. Preserve at all costs your aristocratic tradition, that ruling is the responsibility of the few; but purge it of the corrupting influences, which the industrial revolution brought, by the deliberate formation of a new aristocracy of intellect and character, which will resolutely aim at political power and use it for the enforcement of reason and justice.

This advice is in effect a demand for revolutionary action; for it involves the exclusion from political power of the property owner and of the mass of the people. But it is not revolution of the accepted kind, since it is neither in the interest of the capitalists nor of the proletariat. The Platonic statesman would be equally opposed to the dictatorship of the "haves" and to that of the "have nots," seeing in both the domination of one social group and the perpetuation of the class struggle. Finding his inspiration in the past, he would try to restore the harmony of interests which he would claim existed before the bourgeois revolution, and for this reason he can be called a *conservative revolutionary*. For his aim is at all costs to preserve the *ethos* of the British tradition from the dangers of Liberalism and Fascism and Communism. This *ethos*, he believes, still lives in the hearts of the people, but it has been strangled by the foreign excrescences which the industrial revolution plastered over it. These he must tear off, in order that the true spirit of the community can flourish again. But political and economic revolution is not enough. After any such violent changes, it is only a matter of time before the new Government begins to abuse its power. There never has been and never will be a revolution which did not teem with good intentions and inaugurate a new era of social justice. But once the transference of power has been accomplished and a new class has occupied the seat of government, a change occurs. The economic advantages of political control become apparent to the new rulers, their good intentions are forgotten, and the common man to whom freedom was promised finds himself enslaved once more. Revolution therefore is waste of time and human life, unless it is accompanied by a change in the men who make it, as well as in the institutions they control.

To change men is far more difficult than to change institutions. For the latter can be destroyed and rebuilt by the application of force, the former cannot. Man cannot be forced to be good: he can only be trained and persuaded and cajoled into seeing the folly of his ways. A statesman can draft a law and publish it: he can even compel men to obey it. But he himself is under no such compulsion, and it is the maker of laws who must be just and honest if a constitution is to work. On his morality depends the happiness of the community, and unless he freely accepts the commands of justice, he will be a tyrant, and not a true ruler.

But the moral code is not purely a matter for the individual will, nor is the individual entirely free to accept or to reject it. He is himself a product of it, and conditioned by the institutions of the society in which he lives. The human soul is not a mysterious force with a life of its own, floating in a spiritual ether outside the everyday world of action, every now and then darting down to assert, "This is right and that is wrong," but a member of that world, conditioned by it and conditioning it too. We are both creatures and creators of our environment, and freedom is just the consciousness of this fact and the understanding of its implications. I am not free to jump thirty feet across a river: the laws of gravity and the structure of my body limit my freedom. But I am free to study the workings of nature and to build a bridge across which I can safely walk. Again, I am not free to renounce the morality of my home and country and civilization; I cannot do it because it is part of my personality and a mainspring of my will. But I am free to study that morality, to analyse its implications, and in the light of that knowledge to try to modify it and redirect it in the direction which I think right.

This understanding and redirection of current morality must be undertaken if any political revolution is to achieve success. The statesmen must change not only the constitution and laws and economic system, but also the moral and social institutions by which men live. For the former must ultimately conform to the latter. If the ruling class behave aggressively and self-assertively in their private lives, and their moral code encourages such behaviour, then no political reform will permanently prevent war; instead, social habits will modify the political institutions to suit themselves. If the acquisitive instinct is stimulated by religion or morality, then no Communist society will remain Communist for long: property will make its appearance in some form or other.

The Platonic statesman therefore, like the modern Communist, cannot admit that private life and morality are the concern only of the individual. For him there is no distinction of self-regarding and other-regarding actions. The most intimate secrets of private life must be opened to him and he must analyse and direct them in the proper way.

If we ask what are the most important elements in our private life, there can be no real doubt of the correct answer. Marriage and the family are the central institutions of all human societies. They engage our attention for more hours a day than anything perhaps except our work: they are the cause of more happiness and misery than any other single factor, and lastly, they are the thread upon which the future of the race depends. They are therefore the first institutions which we must analyse, trying both to discover their *raison d'être* and to consider the part they must play in the social order.

Plato's attitude to them was as simple as it was

revolutionary. With the Greek city-state in mind, he proposed their total abolition for all members of the ruling *élite*. No ruler in his State is allowed to be a husband or a wife. The men and women will live together in common barracks, without privacy and on perfectly equal terms. Permanent relationships between them will be forbidden as absolutely as free love. There will be neither promiscuity nor marriage, because they will all be so intent on the work of government and the discovery of truth that they cannot be allowed to waste time on personal relations.

But children will be needed for the State, and so regular religious festivals will be arranged where those suitable and eugenically fit will be brought together. On these occasions special privileges will be granted to those who have distinguished themselves in battle or in public service, and so it will be ensured that the best citizens produce most children. Women will be allowed to mate between twenty and forty, men between twenty-five and fifty-five, but no permanent relations may be entered into. They must meet once only in the sacred festival and then depart upon their respective businesses.

When the child is born it will be taken from its mother and brought up in a State nursery. The mother may come to suckle it, but the greatest care is taken to prevent her recognizing her own child, for all the rulers are one family and the mother must regard all children as equally hers. So, too, with the children: they must never know who their parents are, but treat all the elders of the ruling class as fathers and mothers, all their contemporaries as brothers and sisters. For they are to be trained to be not private citizens with private interests, but public servants caring only for the State.

That, in short, is Plato's revolutionary plan for the ideal relationship of man to woman and of parent to child. But he did not propose it for the man in the street, any more than he proposed the abolition of private property for him. The subject classes were to be allowed everything a man could wish—except self-government. Only the members of the ruling class were to have no property, no wives or husbands and no families, and Plato gave three reasons for this strange regulation of the rulers' life. In the first place he argued that if a man really cares about his job he will not want to be distracted by marriage or by children. Love and marriage are two of the most disturbing things in life. They take up a great deal of time and they are an interruption to any profession or trade. The more wrapped up he is in his job the more a man tends to neglect his family, and Plato argued that if he is really interested in the work for its own sake, then he will not want to be distracted by wife or children. In the case of civilians the distractions will not matter so much, because they are under the absolute dictatorship of the ruling class. The lovelorn farmer or the banker who is too much of a family man can be kept up to scratch by Government control. But there is no one to supervise the ruling *élite*, and so they must be relieved of these distractions. The ruler must not be a breadwinner or a family man: he must be interested in philosophy to the exclusion of everything else; and if he is, then he will not want, and must not be allowed to have, a wife and family.

When Plato abolished marriage and the family he was not preaching a doctrine of free love and easy morals. He was demanding a more rigid self-control for his ruling class than the ordinary man can achieve. His ideal was not unlike that of the monk or priest who takes vows of celibacy and tries to sublimate his earthly emotions and his human love into love of God and service to the community. But the Platonic ruler differs from the monk in two particulars. Firstly, he considers the future: he sees that if no one marries there will be no children; and since the rulers are the pick of the population it is their duty to have as many children as is consistent with their efficiency as rulers. So Plato advocated not celibacy for his rulers, but eugenics, the breeding of children as carefully as horses or dogs are bred to-day, and with as little personal interest in the woman or the child as the expert horse breeder feels in his horses. The really responsible citizen, says Plato, must not produce children just to satisfy a personal whim or to please someone he or she is in love with. The children must be produced for the State, and according to scientific principles of breeding. They are not to be mere products of love, or by-products of personal pleasures. Child-bearing is, in fact, a duty, like soldiering or administering the State, and must be strictly regarded as such. That is the first difference between the morality of Plato's ruler and that of the monk or the Catholic priest.

In the second place, Plato did not believe that

human love or physical passion were in themselves wicked as some religious people are inclined to believe. No Greek could believe the body evil: the Greeks knew more of its beauty than any other nation, and human love seemed to them the most natural thing in the world, with its natural expression in physical emotion. Plato was a moralist but he was not a Puritan, and he saw no reason to forbid his rulers the pleasures of physical intercourse any more then he forbade them the pleasures of physical exercise or of food and drink. Such pleasures, in his view, do no harm in their proper place; they are not in themselves wicked: but they are wrong if they distract rulers from their work. So love and physical emotion were permissible in his view if they were kept strictly on a level with other physical emotions, if, in fact, they were depersonalized and given no continuity or permanence. Plato would not have minded his rulers liking nice furniture or beautiful buildings: only they must not want to possess them. So, too, with human love: if it was treated as a passing pleasure, like a glass of good wine, Plato would have found it wholesome: but if it meant falling in love with someone, wanting to be with her always, missing her when she was away, worrying whether she cared for you, and so on—then Plato would have said it had become a distraction and must be forbidden to the man whose work was ruling.

For this reason, if for no other, Plato would have welcomed the invention of contraceptives and encouraged their use among his *élite*. For the contraceptive emphasizes the distinction between the two

aspects of sex as an expression of love and as a
means of procreation. By decreasing anxiety with
regard to childbirth, it allows a more carefree
pleasure in the sexual act and enables man to plan
the breeding of children scientifically. Plato had
admitted the use of abortion to destroy children produced by women too old for perfect childbearing,
and since he encouraged his rulers after a certain age to
be free in their sexual intercourse provided they did
not lose interest in their work, the contraceptive
would have seemed to him an instrument by the use
of which reason can control matter and still further
depersonalize the sexual act.

This brings us to Plato's second reason for forbidding marriage and the family to his ruling class. Falling in love, he argued, and wanting a family are really
expressions of the acquisitive instinct. He had forbidden his ruling class any form of property whatsoever, and so he argued that marriage and the family,
which are really a sort of property, must be forbidden
to them too. The love of man for woman is based
on a longing for ownership and pride of possession.
Each in their own way, husband and wife regard
each other as a possession to be jealously guarded.
Each of them usually dislikes it if the other shows
too much interest in the opposite sex. Why is this
unless their feelings are fundamentally possessive?
We tend to think of the lover as a romantic figure
full of self-sacrifice and devotion. Plato thought he
was far more concerned with getting hold of something he wanted, enjoying it in private and enjoying
the fact that no one else could share his enjoyment.

Human love between man and woman was in his view a sort of mutual ownership which built a wall round the two people and cut them off from other people.

And the same in Plato's view applies to the family. It is an exclusive organization, a private world into which we try to escape, and in the security of which we seek comfort and satisfaction. Even if we do make sacrifices for our children's education and feel ourselves highly magnanimous in doing so, we do it because they are *our* children and we are proud of *our* productions. A man will sacrifice time and money for his garden, to make it beautiful: a woman may expend hours on improving her appearance. They would not claim to be disinterested in doing either of these things. But is not their attitude to their children very much the same? They want the children to be successes, not really for the children's sake, but because the children belong to them and they want their children to win the prizes of life in competition against their neighbours'.

Plato thought this exclusive sense of property was an inevitable accompaniment to marriage, and that for this reason marriage was just as dangerous to the ruler as property. It would corrupt his loyalty to the State and give him a private interest which would distract him from his job. For Plato was a revolutionary; he wanted his pupils to be men who could work miracles and change the world: and he thought that the only people that really change the world are the people who have no feeling for private property as such, even wives or children. Four hundred and

fifty years later Jesus was to urge the same thing to
His chosen apostles. He, too, insisted that they should
give up father and mother and family—everything
for His sake. But like Plato He realized this vocation
could only be for the *few*, and added the text: "He
that is able to receive it, let him receive it." Everyone is not capable of the supreme sacrifice. The
real revolutionary, the man or woman who is to
transform the world, must put his work first and his
friends second. He must renounce them, not grudg-
ingly with a feeling of loss, but gladly, because he
cares for something infinitely more valuable. He
cannot have friends or family in the usual sense of
the word because he is so intent upon achieving his
ideal of human society that he has no time or interest
for individual human beings. In his personal relations
he will probably seem cold and inhuman, irresponsible
and changeable, as if he did not care about any
human being at all. Caring only about humanity,
his love for that excludes all other love.

In the third place Plato argued that marriage must
involve an inferior status for women. In the Athens
of his day it was little more than the purchase by the
man of a chattel to manage his household and bear
him children. The wife was economically dependent
on her husband, she had no political rights, and she
was not given any education. She was not even a
labourer since she received no wages and had no
defence against exploitation, but a bondservant at
the mercy of her parents as to whom she married,
of her husband when she was married. Plato could
not permit such slaves to be members of his ruling

class and to live with his *élite*. His ruling class demanded women who were the equal of their men,
and he saw that if they are to be this then they cannot be relegated to the home. He did not deny that
most women are physically weaker than men, and
he also believed that they were intellectually inferior.
But he did not think that a sufficient reason for con-
fining all women to the home and refusing them
citizen rights. He claimed, instead, that the best
women should be educated exactly as the best men
are educated. In his ruling class there was to be no
differential treatment of the sexes at all. They were
to live together and even to fight together on terms of
absolute equality.

It is one of the ironies of history that the phrase
"Platonic love" should have come to mean a spiritual
relationship devoid of physical desire. Such love, in
Plato's view, was fit only for God, and he never
advocated it between his citizens. He assumed that
human beings will express the love they feel for
one another, and it was in an effort to raise the level
of that love from self-assertion to partnership that he
abolished marriage. The inferior place of women in
Greece had resulted in the assumption by men of
culture that true love could only be felt by man
for man. Homosexual relationships were regarded
as nobler than marriage, and Socrates, though
he disapproved of certain forms of perversion,
had always regarded his marriage and family as
civic duties, inferior in value to his friendships with
young men. Thus the Greek ideal of chivalry
often became homosexual in character—the love

of the adult for the boy, not the love of man for woman.

Plato remained at heart a Greek. The ideal for him was the love of man for man, and his two-fold aim was to purify homosexual relationships of their physical brutalities and at the same time to raise the relationship of man and woman to the homosexual level. Men were to treat women as they treated boys, and to forget as far as possible that they bore children. His rulers should fall in love with one another, disregarding their differences of sex, man with man or woman with woman or man with woman. They should not take these affairs too seriously or become wrapped up in the physical side, but should regard the physical desires as minor pleasures, compared to the real delights of companionship and co-operation and intellectual discussion.

For he was convinced that love is the basis of true philosophy. A true friendship will start on the physical plane and should not be thwarted on that plane. But soon it will transcend the body and, as it matures, will become the co-operation of equals in the achievement of a common purpose. The lovers will feel themselves rivals in their life's work, encouraging and helping and competing with one another, and finally they will find the consummation of desire in dialectic, the discussion and philosophizing which alone can attain truth. With this inspiration, the lovers cease to be "in love," since their love is now centred on truth, and they will regard sexual satisfaction as "play" and relaxation from the enterprise which they share.[1]

[1] See the speech of Diotima in the *Symposium*.

Thus Plato was forced to deny that sex differentiation is in any way fundamental, in order to maintain that Reason, the immortal part of the soul, is shared by men and women alike. If woman is not to be relegated to the Mohammedan level, she must be held capable of philosophy, and her sexual differences regarded as accidental to her true nature. In that case, the distinction of normal and perverse relations is unreal, since the friendship of two rational beings is equally good, to whichever sex they belong. It is only when we descend to the utilitarian level and consider the procreation of children, that sex difference becomes important; but here love must cease, to be replaced by civic obligation and the iron discipline of eugenic law.

The abolition of marriage was a tremendous assertion of the rights of woman. It raised her to the level of man, and it postulated her rational nature. But it has never been kindly received by Plato's readers, who are often shocked by its "immorality," its equanimity in the face of perversion, and its clear separation of sexual pleasure from procreation. Plato knew that this would happen. Recognizing the strength of *tabu* and superstition, he put it forward in a very tentative fashion, but there is no part of his writing which surpasses this passage[1] in its style, imagination, or philosophical clarity. In the face of every instinct and prejudice, he was clear-sighted enough to see that, if women were the equals of men, and to be treated as such, then sexual morality must be drastically altered and marriage and the family, in

[1] See *Republic* Book **V**.

the form in which he knew them, must be abolished.

But can you free women from their bondage? Plato thought it was only possible for a select few. Most women are happiest uneducated and doing the work of the home, just as most men are happiest in the security of subjection to dictatorship. But the women of the ruling class, if they are to be worthy partners of the men and produce worthy children, must be free, and to achieve this Plato saw no other way open than to abolish marriage and the family. It was essential for man and woman alike. Given marriage, he said, man will always be the dominant partner, the possessor, woman the passive recipient, the possessed. And she will compensate for this inferior position by accentuating her sexual charms and becoming the possessor in matters of physical emotion. She will spend time and money on making herself beautiful and attractive, and she will long for the power over men which those attractions afford. Plato was a feminist not only in the sense that he wanted to free the best women from the bondage of the family; he also wanted to free them from the ambitions which that bondage imposed on them.

It is often said that women are more influenced than men by consideration of persons. They think in terms of people, not of programmes and ideas, and they accept ideas not because they are true, but because those ideas are associated in their minds with male admirers. Plato would argue that this was due to their inferior position. They never can get away from personal relations because they are economically and mentally dependent on men. And so their whole ambitions are concentrated either on captivating men or on making their children into successes. To free them from these narrow ambitions, to get them to look beyond persons to ideas, and to give them real intellectual and moral independence, he was willing to abolish the home, and he argued that most women would not like this at all. They would not be willing to surrender the power which physical charm gives them, or to be treated by men exactly as though they were colleagues of slightly inferior ability. They would feel slighted and disappointed when they could no longer rely on the chivalry and romantic love of the dominant male. But women, in Plato's view, cannot have it both ways: they cannot break up the home and demand perfect equality and then use that equality merely to further their womanly ambitions. And for this reason only a woman who is prepared to be treated as a colleague and fellow-worker would be allowed to be a member of his ruling class. If the woman wants to rely on her charms, then she must accept the inferior position and the inferior responsibilities of home life. She can enjoy either the chivalry of men or equality with men, but she cannot have both.

It is not sufficient to treat this theory with disgust and ridicule, or to assert that it is the product of the perversions of a degenerate age and therefore has no applicability to-day. Modern feminist movements have nearly always urged the complete equalization of the sexes, and advocated the opening of all professions to women. Claiming that women are "as good" as men, they have tried to break down all the ties which bind women to home and husband, and have often advocated a free and voluntary partnership of the sexes. Their propaganda has taken the line that women should be allowed to behave as men behave, not that women should be free to develop their special talents. And for this reason women's education and sport have been definitely modelled on that of men, notwithstanding the fact that on these lines women as a whole are usually inferior to men. We have only to examine the European university to see that Plato's arguments are still the assumptions of feminism and of advanced educational theory.

But modern theory has not often seen as clearly as Plato the consequences of this assumption. If the proper place of woman in society is alongside man, if there is no distinction of civic function between them, and the "good life" is identical for both sexes, then the chief justification of marriage as a permanent union disappears. Two men may be good friends and decide to live together, but it would be fantastic for them to consummate a permanent union: why, then, should the bond between a man and a woman, each devoted to his or her professional work, be inviolable provided that, with the aid of scientific technique, they produce no children, or alternatively that the State takes over the education of the family? And secondly, if woman like man is to put her profession first and her home second, can it still be asserted that the home is the best place for the upbringing of children at all? The justification for the home as the educational centre disappears when woman regards it as the place of relaxation from her daily work.

Whether we like it or no, the equalization of the sexes must seek to approximate the life of women to that of men, if for no other reason because men *have* dominated society and male activity and education have been the model of feminist agitation. There is no special function for women in society, apart from the care of children and home, because there never has been: and therefore feminism is the assertion by the inferior sex that she *can* live a man's life nearly as well as men. By this assertion woman denies her differences and special excellences, and is content to "play second fiddle" to the dominant male, as boys ape their adult idols. And so the attempt to demand "equality of status" confirms woman in an inferior position, making her the weaker competitor in a race she must always lose. The chivalry which men felt for a sex which, in spite of its physical and theoretical inferiority, could do many things better than they, is replaced by a kindly sympathy and encouragement for a weaker rival. And conversely the marriage partnership in which a man's capacities were increased by his wife's personal help and encouragement, so that she, as a woman, actually contributed something to his work which no man could give, is turned into an unequal rivalry, with all the friction that rivalry must bring. The failure of many modern marriages must be attributed to Platonic ideals: and the decrease in the birth-rate is due not so much to the introduction of

contraceptives, as to their use by women in order
to liberate themselves from the bondage of the family.
Contraceptives have never stopped a mother from
having a family if she wanted to have one: to her
they are only a god-given method of protecting
her family's best interests from the sexual passion of
the unruly male.

Plato faces us with the full problem of "feminism."
Granted the initial assumption that woman to be free
must adopt the life of man, he shows (1) that in this
case she is likely to be a weaker rival, (2) that the
care of children must be taken from her, and (3) that
in a society of free men and women sexual pleasure
and child-bearing will be divorced from one another.
The former will become an individual gratification
of private desire, the latter a civic obligation whose
control can only be entrusted to the State. But he also
shows that this new form of society will only survive
if it can introduce a new self-control and a new
sexual morality. Men and women may declare themselves "equal" and proclaim that the old era of male
possession and female slavery is closed. Such declara-
tions will have no effect against deep-seated habits
so long as permanent marriage-unions are retained.
For sexual passion is possessive and jealous. The lover,
so long as he is in love, wants some sort of "permanent" union. If, therefore, woman claims equality
of opportunity in a society where the institution of
marriage is still preserved, the result will be not the
depersonalization of sexual relations, but an intensifi-
cation of the romantic bond. There will be more
divorces—but while they last marriages will be more

passionate and more jealous than before. Sex will become a dominant fact in social life, disturbing the efficiency of the worker even more than before. For, although the social utility of marriage will have been destroyed, the institution will remain as a justification and an incentive to possessiveness and jealousy. To equalize the sexes, while retaining the institutions of marriage and the family, is in Plato's view to have the worst of two contrasted moral systems.

This would be Plato's judgment on our age, and on our astonishing obsession with sexual problems. He would not call us really equal, since equality of the sexes, in his view, can only be achieved where passion is depersonalized, and false romance suppressed by the abolition of all permanent unions. The justification for permanent marriage was the existence of the family. When this is gone, sexual possessiveness and marriage have no social utility, and the former becomes the jealous passion of a child shouting that no one shall share its toys. The idea that either man or woman has the right to enjoy friendship as a private pleasure, where there is no social justification for this privacy, would repel Plato, just as it would repel him if a man claimed to exclude everyone from his property, when he was not working on it or enriching the community with its produce. Marriage, like private ownership, when it ceases to be socially beneficial, becomes a social disease.

And so we are faced with a tragic dilemma. If woman is to be free and gain the status of man, then sexual possessiveness—and marriage with it— must be suppressed. If, on the other hand, we value the institution of the family and doubt our powers to change the deep-seated instincts of sexual life, then woman must renounce the status of man and retain the marriage partnership as the chief function of her life. There is only one way out of this dilemma and Plato took it. He suggested that some men and women are capable of a higher morality, but most are not. If we follow Plato, however, we must face the fresh problem which a differential morality brings, and devise a legal system under which there is one code for the *élite* and another for the common people.

Plato would suggest that we had almost reached this stage to-day without realizing it. We are divided into the emancipated and the traditionally minded, but the emancipated are not aware of their responsibilities. They are content to use the scientific discoveries of birth-control for the gratification of personal pleasure, and to pour an easy ridicule on the superstitious folly and brutalities of the conservative majority. They claim that they alone are free and reasonable: but although they renounce the old morality, they are enslaved by their own obsessions and refuse to subject themselves voluntarily to the sterner discipline which true equality demands. They do not realize that the common man may, in fact, be happier and contented to remain "brutal" and "uncivilized," because they forget that the social and economic conditions of his life are vastly different from their own leisured and wealthy freedom. The instability and unhappiness of modern life arise chiefly on Plato's view from this irresponsibility of the leisured intelligentsia whose reason is employed, not on the constructive task of discovering the new self-discipline which a changing world demands, but in ridiculing an institution whose social utility they disregard.

Plato would have cited Soviet Russia as an example of this false Liberalism with regard to morality, a crude misapplication of his own theory to modern life. Basing themselves on the philosophy of Marx, the Communists urged that to reform society they must reform private morality as well. They, too, broke up the home because it made woman the bond-servant of man and because children should be the possession not of the parents but of the State. Encouraging women to work as the equals of men, they made State *crèches* and nurseries where the children could be left while the parents were at work, and they enabled men and women to get divorced as easily as we allow them to get married. They did this not because they disbelieved in morality and convention, but because they wanted to abolish private ownership by one person of another person's life. They argued that if you disapprove of the private ownership of the means of production, because it puts the worker at the mercy of the employer, then you must also disapprove of marriage because it makes women and children dependent on the whims and fancies of the father. And so the Russian revolution was not only an experiment in economic planning, but also an experiment in a new social morality and a new relationship of man to woman and of parents to children.

But there is one difference between the Communist attitude to the family and that which Plato advocated. Just as Plato was content to leave most people their private property, so he was content to leave most people their family life. His Communism was a Communism of the *élite*. There, as everywhere else, the Russians have been more democratic. Their Communism is for everyone, just as their education is for everyone, and so they made their new social morality a universal code, and tried to free all the women of Russia from what they called the servitude of marriage. The freedom which Plato thought that only a select few would appreciate was given by the Communists to every citizen of the Union of Soviet Socialist Republics.

Long ago, in 1848, Karl Marx wrote a warning which his followers left unheeded. He said that if we merely abolish the restraints and restrictions of marriage we break down morality and level human life down to the standard of the beast. By giving men and women absolute freedom in their sexual life we let lust and greed run rampant, and women who were previously the private property of men become the public property of all who care to use them. Their position is worse than before: for now they are the common spoil of the whole community.

Something very like this did happen in the early years of the revolution. An old morality was abolished and in its place came a freedom which the ordinary man and woman were not strong enough to enjoy. A few idealists in Russia did not abuse their new freedom: the common man either abused it or disliked it, and in the last year or two the Russians have been trying to build up a new code of social morality. Wanton promiscuity and frequent divorce are frowned upon: parents are held responsible for their children. It is clear already from the Russian experiment that to abolish the home is to expect a standard of conduct far too high for the common man, and on this point Plato's pessimism has been justified. What measures should be taken in our own country, and how far Plato's analysis can be usefully employed, I must leave the reader to decide.

WAS Plato a Communist? No question is more often or more unprofitably discussed by political philosophers and by students of Plato. On the one hand it is argued that his ruling *élite*, forbidden to enjoy the pleasures of wealth and marriage, was the first example of a communist society; on the other, that since Plato permitted the vast majority of the population to have property, wife, and children, he can be exonerated from the charge of being the father of Communist theory. Both contentions are equally futile. Plato was a Greek, not a modern European: a citizen of a city-, not of a nation-state. The social and economic problems which confronted him were those of a mercantile civilization based on small-scale industries and craft skills, utterly different from the gigantic factories and machine techniques of modern capitalism: and lastly, he was brought up to assume slave labour as an integral part of the economic order.

These three differences make it utterly impossible for Plato to have elaborated a Communist philosophy. Communism, the product of an era of international trade which seemed to link the world into a single economic system, is a universal doctrine and looks forward to a world-order and to the destruction of national states: the product of an era of expanding productivity and wealth, it aims at procuring for the working classes the full fruits of their labours: the product of the exploitation of free labour, it looks to the control by the people of the economic and political system. In each of these three particulars Plato's philosophy differs profoundly from that of Marx; he looks forward not to a world order but to a regenerate city-state: he seeks to redeem the working classes not from economic but from political exploitation and, because he accepted slavery, he could never envisage the control of the political system by all "the workers." The place of slavery in Greek civilization has often been over-emphasized and misinterpreted. It is simply untrue to suggest that the city-state was based upon cheap slave labour, or that its citizens were a leisured class living off the labour of serfs. There was a working class in Athens, as there is a working class in America; indeed, the position of the slave in the former case was not unlike that of the negro in the latter: he did not drive the citizen from the labour market, but competed with him, forced down his standard of living, and reduced his wages.

We may press the analogy still further. The Greek slave was not entirely without rights: he could bring an action for outrage against his master in the courts, he received pay for his work, he could purchase his liberty, and even be granted citizenship for public services: the negro in America or South Africa is scarcely in a better position. Like the negro, he was generally a "barbarian" and employed on unskilled or semi-skilled work in factories, in the mines, and, above all, in domestic service: but if he showed intelligence he could advance to positions of considerable responsibility. Lastly, his social degradation was defended, even by thinkers such as Aristotle, in much the same way as negro oppression is defended to-day.

The effect of slavery on Greek social development was most profound in mercantile cities such as Corinth or Athens, which depended for their food supplies and raw materials on the export trade. Here, from the beginning of the fifth century, industry and mass-production began to flourish. Factories with twenty or thirty hands were not uncommon, and we hear of a shield factory which employed one hundred and twenty slaves. But the free crafts-man, the peasant, and even the free labourer, were at first so little threatened that Athens could welcome new citizens and resident foreigners in large numbers. The reason for this is two-fold. In the first place, since there was no industrial machinery, mass-production could only be employed on a limited number of products: in the second, the ownership of slaves was only remunerative where demand was constant—free labour can be set off at slack periods, slaves cannot—and it was only open to the rich with capital to invest. For those who could afford it, it was a profitable investment, calculated to bring a return of over 30 per cent.

But although skilled craftsmen could always hold their own, wage-rates were bound to be forced down, and it became clear that the steady increase of the citizen population must be checked. In 451 Pericles limited Athenian citizenship to those of Athenian birth on both sides, and six years later, when an Egyptian prince presented the city with forty-five thousand bushels of corn, he struck five thousand names from the roll before distributing the bounty to the citizen population. From now onwards democracy meant not the rule of the proletariat, but of the citizen proletariat, and citizenship became not a right but a privilege. This privilege was enhanced by payment to jurors (in 451) and to the civic militia, and the State was forced to repair the ill-effects of cheap slave labour by doles and bounties and political payments to the citizens. In 432, at the beginning of the great war, the population of Attica consisted approximately of 172,000 citizens, 30,000 resident foreigners, and 115,000 slaves, and since women had no active political rights, the franchise was enjoyed by one-eighth of the whole people. By 323 the position was still worse. Out of a total population of 258,000, there were 112,000 citizens, 42,000 resident aliens, and 104,000 slaves.

The effect of slavery was threefold. By flooding the market with cheap labour, it retarded technological advance and the introduction of science into industry. By threatening the wages of the free workers, it forced down the birth-rate in the class of free citizens, and thirdly, it hampered the spread of equalitarian philosophies and the formation of working-class and Socialist movements.

We must bear this in mind when we ask ourselves what Plato would think of modern Communism, and what criticisms he would make of our economic system. For Plato was oblivious to the problem of slavery. In the *Laws* he accepted it as an awkward but necessary fact; in the *Republic* he refers to it only when he suggests that Greeks should not enslave Greek prisoners of war. Otherwise he blithely disregarded it and built his society on a basis of free citizen labour, with slaves only for domestic use, thereby implying that the ideal State would not be a mercantile city with a great export trade, but an agricultural community, living on its own resources and exporting only its surplus produce. Thus he refused to face the real problem of Greek civilization, whose highest cultural level was always to be found precisely in those mercantile cities whose slave economy he tacitly rejected; and he limited his criticisms and proposals to the reorganization of a privileged citizen body, disregarding the majority of human beings who fell outside this category.

It is already clear that Plato would not be in sympathy with modern Socialism, which is based on the two demands for economic justice and for workers' control. While admitting the obvious fact of the failure of capitalism to achieve its objective—the maximization of wealth—he would argue that Socialists, by concentrating their attack upon economic injustice, have blinded themselves to the real problem, and by demanding workers' control are heading for catastrophe. Workers' control might possibly be no worse than capitalist control, but on the other hand it is not likely to be much better if the workers' ideal is no different from that of the capitalist whom he is to supplant. What object can there be, he would ask, in undergoing the horrors of revolution in order that a new ruling class may gain power whose only motive is material gains and which demands freedom only to enjoy the pleasures of prosperity? Socialism might succeed in distributing wealth more "fairly": it might even increase productivity, but it could not eradicate the fundamental evil that power is permitted to rest in the hands of "civilians" whose only aim is worldly happiness. Socialism is the creed of one side in the class-war and for this reason it cannot overcome it. For the fundamental fault lies not in the capitalist system as such, but in the hearts of the individual men and women of whom that system is made up. If their hearts can be changed, and their intelligence properly disciplined, then the system will right itself and become not the master whom the statesman must obey, but the servant of the philosopher-king.

For this reason Plato would feel only disgust for the Communist glorification of material and technological advance. The worship of machine power and of natural science would seem to him merely vulgar, and he would laugh at the self-complacency with which Russia asserts that she is outstripping her capitalist rivals. Plato was not an opponent of applied science: he would have encouraged any research which increased man's control over nature and thus contributed to the happiness and security of the civilian population. Believing that it is the purpose of the State to make men happy, he was bound to welcome scientific advances which really contributed to that end. But for him the chief virtue of science was not its practical application: pure science, the disinterested search for truth, was an end in itself, and the real scientist was the man who pursued truth to the exclusion of all other interests. The philosopher must always be a pure scientist in this sense and prefer knowledge to material happiness, whereas the civilian sees only the material benefits which science can give.

Plato would not therefore object to the Communist's belief in science as such, but to his stress on its utilitarian aspect. He would be pleased to see the possibilities of material happiness steadily increasing under the Five Year Plan, but he would ask why the ruling class seemed as pleased as their subjects with these advances. It is not, he would argue, the function of government to make men rich, but to make them good, and it is therefore no proof of the excellence of Communism that it can outdo capitalism in the production of wealth. Wealth is as great an evil as poverty, and a Government which encourages people to think in terms of wealth is sowing the seeds of a new class-war. Granted that Russia grows really wealthy, how can a people, taught to regard material success as the highest end, fail to be divided against itself and to break up into factions each claiming a larger share of the booty? How can it fail to become imperialist and seek to exploit the natural resources of others? And lastly, how can its rulers, who extol material success, avoid the corruption of their own motives and the secret pursuit of personal gain?

We shall return later to this criticism of Communist ideals, but already we can observe that Plato would consider Russian Communism as an attempt to impose the standards of Western civilization on a barbarian country, arguing that, for all their differences of political organization, Russia and America are linked by the tie of a common aim. They are societies dominated by the acquisitive instinct. Their ideals are those of the technicians and craftsmen and bankers, whom he had relegated to his third class; their philosophy of life is materialistic and anti-religious, suppressing the spirit of true philosophy—the search for the eternal principles of human conduct—and enslaving reason to material progress. Giving the highest place to natural science and the conquest of nature, they put power into the hands of men who have not duly considered the ends for which power should be used. Just as American Republicanism is the philosophy of the privileged classes, who enjoy the benefits of the industrial revolution, so Communism is the creed of the outcasts and exploited, who claim their share of the wealth. Both of them are products of the acquisitive instinct.

The difference between industrial democracy and the Communist State lies therefore not in their ends, but in their methods, and Plato might well suggest that, whereas the former cannot obtain permanent success, the latter can, since it is the wholehearted and scientific application of reason to the maximization of wealth. Russia and America are both devoted to this end, but Communism, because it has articulated its principles and become fully self-conscious of its nature, will succeed where America will fail. If material progress is accepted as the only end of man—and this is the underlying assumption not only of Marxism but of Liberal democracy—then, in a society based on free labour and not on slavery, the Communist State is the only proper form of political and economic organization. Any other system will lead to slumps and economic disturbances which will hinder the march of material progress. Communism therefore is Liberalism purified of its inconsistencies and sentimentalities—the theology of collective wealth—and as such it is the fiercest enemy of true philosophy.

But in spite of condemning its ideals, Plato would be passionately interested in the Russian experiment, just because it is a self-conscious attempt to plan human society in accordance with a clear philosophy of life. Communist philosophy may be wrong, but it is a philosophy; and the rulers of Russia are indeed philosopher-kings who have organized their State on clear-cut philosophical principles. For this reason Plato would find much to praise in the political and social structure of the U.S.S.R.

Above all, he would admire the organization of the Communist Party, an *élite* trained for public service, subjected to military discipline, and schooled to accept without question the philosophy and the policy of its leaders. The party member is the political soldier of Communism, who sees to it that throughout the length and breadth of the land the plans of the philosopher-kings are carried out by the subject classes. His task demands two qualities, courage and obedience—the willingness to die for beliefs accepted on trust from the few who know. Plato in the Academy had sought to train "administrators" of this sort, and the programme for their education which he sketched in the *Republic*[1] could be accepted without demur by any Russian educationalist. He, too, had seen that the heroic self-sacrifice and asceticism which such public service demands, can only be found in a select and highly trained *élite*, inspired by a great idea, for the sake of which they are glad to sacrifice their own lives, as well as the lives of others. In Communist Russia he would have seen the tyranny of just such an idea and it would have confirmed his own belief that real civil courage is only granted to the fanatic who is so convinced of the rightness of his plan that he cares more for the idea of human happiness and justice than for actual happiness and actual justice. For the sake of the Five Year Plan, the Communist is willing to impose hardship and even death upon his fellow-workers. His eyes are fixed on their future happiness, so he can cheerfully neglect their present sufferings.

Here, then, Plato would find a resemblance between his own ideal State and Communist Russia. Both are attempts to make life conform to a strictly rational pattern, which the philosopher believes essential for human happiness; and to impose this pattern of life, government is placed in the hands of an *élite* trained to obey the philosophers' commands. But the resemblance does not stop there. Plato would have agreed with the Communist that it is quite useless to entrust the lives of men and women to the care of any picked body of rulers, however pure their

[1] The reference is to Books II–IV. The education of philosophers in Books VI–VII must be sharply distinguished. Here, of course, there is no analogy with Soviet methods.

motives, if you allow any vested interest to flourish unchecked. No combination of citizens intent on their own economic ends must be allowed to threaten or cajole the government, whether it be a company anxious to increase its profits or a trade union formed to protect the standard of living of the poorer classes. Every vested interest is a danger to good government, and there is no way of preventing their influence except to abolish them altogether. Plato and Lenin were both prepared to do this.

There is, indeed, a deep similarity between the temper of the two philosophers. They both held that philosophy and science cannot be permitted to stand aside from life and contemplate the scene. Philosophy must leave the Academy and capture power if human happiness is to be achieved. Plato believed the philosopher must become king: Lenin achieved it. It was the belief in the practicability of philosophy which made both of them so ruthless in the use of force. Those qualities in Communism which shock us most, its suppression of the opposition, its sacrifice of the individual life to the great plan, its hostility to all rival creeds, are the qualities which Plato would have most admired. They are qualities of a philosophy which knows exactly what life should be, and regards as bigoted superstitions all religions and philosophies which differ from it. Neither Plato nor Lenin would have hesitated to order the death penalty for heresy and deviations: and their apparent inhumanity was due to their complete certainty of the righteousness of their cause and the truth of their philosophy. Both claimed that merciless austerity would in the long run prove itself merciful. If surgery is needed, it is not mercy but fear which prompts us to put aside the knife.

Two objections will be raised to this analogy between Plato and Lenin. In the first place, it seems blatantly to contradict an earlier assertion that, on Plato's view, Communism is essentially a materialist and acquisitive philosophy; and in the second place, it is at variance with Lenin's own doctrine of the dictatorship of the proletariat. The answers to these objections will perhaps clarify the Platonic attitude to Communism.

Let us begin with the second. The philosophy of Marx and Lenin was based on the observed fact of class-conflict and class-domination, and the theoretical conclusion that the dictatorship of the proletariat will in the end abolish class-conflict. Communism holds that the class-war will develop until either the proletariat seizes power or civilization breaks down, and it therefore asserts that the dictatorship of the proletariat is inevitable if civilization is to survive. But the dictatorship of the proletariat means not that each proletarian should be his own king and govern himself as he did at Athens, but that the Government should serve the interests of the proletariat and suppress their oppressors. For this to be achieved, government must be in the hands of "philosophers" with an administrative staff (the Communist Party) and the proletariat must be subjected to a new dictatorship, or ruling class.

On this point there is no real difference between the views of Plato and Lenin. Plato also believed that the government should serve the interest of "the civilians" and be freed from the corrupting influence of "vested interests." But he was philosopher enough to avoid so ambiguous a phrase as the "Dictatorship of the Proletariat," and to admit that in a totalitarian State there are no dictators except the few who control the military and administrative machine. Stalin is as absolute a ruler as any Platonic philosopher-king.

Where Plato and Lenin would part company is in the selection of the ruling class. Lenin made his appeal to the industrial workers and to intellectuals who had thrown in their lot with them, and the Communist leaders were chiefly drawn from these classes. Seeing that a gigantic lever was needed to overthrow the existing order, he appealed to the discontent of the industrial masses on whose work the system depends. Proletarian solidarity was the means he employed for making a revolution and giving power to the Communist philosophers, and picked proletarians were members of his administrative *élite*. But Plato was convinced that the working classes, like everyone else engaged in industry or trade, were incapable of political wisdom. His rulers were to be drawn from the nobility and the landed gentry, and though he did leave room for the promotion of a worker, he considered such cases so unimportant that he made no proper provision for it. He really wanted a *hereditary ruling caste*, and for this reason he condemned general education as destructive of political discipline.

But the difference between Plato and Lenin is not

simply a difference of opinion about the political capacities of the working classes. Even if Plato went to Russia to-day and saw that self-educated working-class people like Stalin can become rulers of one-sixth of the world, he would still have maintained that these were exceptions, and that most people, whatever class they come from, are incapable of political responsibility. He might have been quite willing to draw his ruling caste from the working classes, but he would still have maintained a rigid separation of ruler and subject, and excluded the mass of the people from any share in framing policy. On this point he would have found himself in disagreement with orthodox Communism which denies that the party is a ruling caste and tries to make it a flexible voluntary organization open to anyone with correct views and enthusiasm for public service. Communist theory believes in general education and the participation of every citizen in government, and urges that the Soviet system is specially constructed to attain this end. It denounces the idea of a ruling class and looks forward to a time when all will be fit to govern.

Plato would not, however, pay much attention to the theorist, and would treat him in much the same way as he treated the educationalist in an earlier chapter. "I am content," he would say, "to see the facts as they are. In Russia to-day you have an able statesman in control. He has built up a political machine which is able to crush all rivals, and of the theorists and idealists who once collaborated with him the majority are now dead or in exile. I have every

sympathy with Stalin, and I consider that on his
principles he is fully justified in all that he has done.
Seeing that the 'noble lie' of democracy and proletarian freedom was necessary to unite the people
and to overthrow the Government, he used it at the
proper time. Now that it has served its purpose he
sees clearly that it must be suppressed and that those
innocents who mistook myth for reality must be
quietly put away. He knows that government is an
affair of the few, and that an efficient bureaucracy is
incompatible with popular control. And so, pre-
ferring the wealth of the people to all else, and seeing
that it can only be obtained by the iron discipline of
reason, he rightly denounces as heretical those who
seek to introduce discussion and debate into his
ordered kingdom, and to raise among his subjects
the banner of true democracy and popular control.
For consider what would happen if the people were
to be given any voice in the affairs of State. Faction
and strife would grow, autonomy would be demanded here, expansion there, and worst of all,
the Communist Party, now the obedient and united
instrument of government, would become a vulgar
centre of debate and discussion. Stalin is indeed wise.
If I understand him aright, he will see to it that
education is used to promote not criticism and
creative thought, but efficiency and obedience. Where
he finds revolt, he will ruthlessly crush it: when
myths become awkward he will discard them and
substitute new ones. For he, like Marx and myself,
is imbued with a profound contempt for the stupidity
of the common man, and an equal certainty that he

and his chosen friends alone are in possession of the knowledge which can bring happiness to men.

"Most of all I admire his mastery of propaganda and the sly humour of his employment of the 'noble lie.' Deciding that the time has come to crush all opposition, he first publishes a new and democratic constitution, and then shoots the advocates of freedom. Thus he accomplishes two ends, both establishing a democratic constitution and ensuring that there will be no one to make use of it. In this he shows modesty as well, and that readiness to learn from his enemies which is the mark of a true statesman. Observing the ease with which the ruler of Germany conducts plebiscites and elections and yet ensures that the voting is always correct, he has resolved even to outbid Hitler and to build up the full machinery of representative institutions. He knows that the façade will at once satisfy the people's craving for power, and decently veil from public curiosity the workings of actual government. For he has observed that, where a people is disciplined and has learnt to respect authority, there democracy can safely be allowed, since no one will abuse it without general disapproval; and he has seen how in England a strong social tradition can ensure the position of a ruling class more firmly than force of arms or threats of violence or even a ministry of propaganda. With these examples before him he has decided that the time is ripe for Russia to enter the ranks of the conservative nations which have evolved a stable order of society and a proper dislike of equalitarian sentiment. He will maintain his secret police and his machinery of internal power for some time to come, but I have no doubt that Russia will soon become an industrial nation, richer than all others, less tinged with Radicalism and Liberal licence, and therefore more able to assert her imperial designs against a divided and distracted world.

"But much though I admire Stalin, I must confess that I regard him as the greatest enemy of truth and knowledge. Not only has he false ideals, but he has developed a philosophy to justify them as perverted as it is persuasive. Denying the existence of God and the hope of a future life, he preaches the pursuit of the things of this world, and sees in the freedom to enjoy wealth and honour and power the highest pleasures of man. For him man is an object, the source of whose movements can be found in natural causes, whose ideas are the product of necessity, and whose every action is predictable by scientific law. And so he regards reason as the natural servant of animal desire, and seeks to control nature only to subject it once more to the tyranny of human appetite and greed. Denying the existence of the rational soul, he cannot himself contemplate the reality behind the worldly appearances, or pursue a happiness not of this world but of the next. Through this ignorance of true philosophy he has raised science, which should be the servant of reason, to the throne of reason itself and has proclaimed as the ultimate reality the transient process of history which comes to be and passes away, a chaos of meaningless events.

"The foolish and short-sighted will laugh at my observations and remark that a false philosophy can harm no one; and this will be true as long as philosophy is merely the recreation of the young or the hobby of the old—as it is in England. But Stalin has harnessed a nation to the realization of his philosophy on earth, and now there are millions of human beings who will carry out his will. At present they are pacific and friendly, for Russia has far to go before it has exploited its natural wealth to the full, but the time will come when the lust for power and the greed to subject all men to their plan will grow strong in the rulers. When that time comes only the influence of true philosophy and self-control can restrain the unruly passions. But philosophy will be long since dead and, as in the days of Pericles and of Napoleon, the revolutionary cry for bread and justice will become the imperial demand for power.

"Such is my verdict upon Stalin and upon the future of Russia. But as for the young men and women in your country who become converted to Communism, not because of its materialist ideas or the hope it offers of future prosperity, but owing to a spirit of dissatisfaction with the existing order, and a longing to free their countrymen from bondage and misery—to them I should say: Beware of harnessing your fine ideals to a doctrine which exalts material prosperity and whips up the hatred and greed of an oppressed class. Your ideals will not harmonize with the passions of those whom you would help: and when you have liberated the oppressed, you will find that they in turn become the oppressors. Be clear then in your own minds that in any revolution, political power must be retained by you and your like, if any social improvement is to be gained; and that it will be your first duty to throw into new bondage those whom you have freed, and ruthlessly to suppress the prophets of materialism and hate. Surrender then your illusion that dictatorship is only a step on the way to freedom, and dream no longer that a time will come when the seeds of class-conflict will die and the State can wither away. The common man will always need the discipline of the few and will always abuse political power; because the reason which is within him is not strong, he can never submit himself voluntarily to the rule of law, or enjoy true freedom.

"Your instinct and the teaching of your Churches make you reluctant to admit this fact, which is confirmed daily by common experience. And so you preach the equality of man and dream of a time when the human race will live at peace, each man proceeding upon his appointed way as effortlessly as the divine planets move in their perfect orbits, never crossing one another's paths or failing in their duty, a starry system of rational beings.

"My young friends, that is a noble ideal which I myself share, but do not expect that you will see it here on earth. Perhaps in heaven you will contemplate reality: in this world you must attempt to give to sluggish and reluctant matter a semblance of order and form. You cannot legislate for rational beings, but must be content to compel a stupid race to avoid the worst consequences of its stupidities. For statesmanship, unlike philosophy, is the art of the second best. It aims, not at perfecting man, but at preventing his further deterioration: and the prudent statesman will be content if he can leave his countrymen no worse off than he found them. One of your teachers once said, 'The Kingdom of Heaven is within you.' He was a wise man and he surely meant that perfection can be contemplated by the mind's eye but can never be given earthly form. If you neglect this saying and, believing that man on earth can live the life of gods, encourage your fellow-men in this false hope, for all your religious ideals and good intentions you will end by destroying what little beauty and order we possess.

"Be content then with smaller hopes, separating clearly from one another your religious ideals and your practical aims, and recognizing that perfection is not of this world, but of the next. And at all costs avoid that heresy which teaches that in the history of the human race we may trace a progress from imperfection towards perfection. Your Communism is the product of an age of eager hopes and aspirations which falsely interpreted the discoveries of natural science as signs that the world was evolving towards the good, and that a spirit of reason was directing that evolution. It believed that reason must in the end prevail and that the workings of historical necessity would finally produce the earthly millennium. This belief is an empty delusion which mistakes material progress for spiritual betterment, and increased wealth for an improvement of manners. When I observe you and compare you with my countrymen, I notice many distinctions of convention and habit, and a difference in the importance attached to particular virtues. We prized courage, ingenuity, good taste, and independence of spirit: you Englishmen seem to prefer kindness and honesty. In this you are different but not better than we, and your differences are the result not of your actions but of conditions for the most part outside your control, such as your greater wealth and your mastery of nature. These 'blessings' have softened the struggle for survival and so enabled you to afford a gentle and humanitarian sentiment, and other such luxuries which in our epoch were not permitted. It is no true virtue to live according to the standards of your age and to fulfil the obligations of your social code. Anybody equipped with intellect and a little self-interest would do that! The truly virtuous man is he who has raised himself above habit and convention and by his knowledge has criticized and changed the manners of his fellow-citizens. The history of our race is the sombre tale of how a few good men from time to time have seen a little further than their fellows and rescued them from their misery. But no such improvements are permanent, always the world slips back into self-assertion and greed, reverting from the truth it fears to the half-truths and hypocrisies which are natural to it.

"I lived in a time when the circle of time was moving from good to bad, from order to disorder, from beauty to chaos. The civilization which our fore-fathers had built up was slipping back into barbarism and anarchy. Art was degenerating into prettiness and the old civic virtues were disappearing. A few of us, among them Socrates, understood. We had no illusions that in some distant future man would be perfect and the State would wither away: we only hoped to stop the collapse, seeing that as things grew worse, not less but more force would be necessary to maintain law and order and social security. So I planned my ideal State as a brake on the wheel of time, not as a stage in the progress of man: and when I wished to gaze on perfection, I fixed my eyes on the eternal realities which do not change, and the beauties which cannot fade because they are not of this world, knowing that here at least in pure philosophy I had a friend uncorruptible by the inevitable processes of change and decay.

"When I look on your civilization and observe the rifts which are apparent in it, the uncertainty of its economic order, the dangers of war, and the break-down of religion and morality, I do not feel a stranger. For you too are born into an epoch of dis-solution, and can no longer look forward to the unconquerable march of progress. Try though you may, you cannot believe that next year will show a splendid advance on last, that Providence is on your side, and that you need only lend assistance to the powers of good which by their own propulsion are pressing on towards perfection. And therefore your Communist philosophy which you cling to is out of date, and you no longer believe your own assertion that dictatorship is only a stage on the way to free-dom. You repeat the slogans and the catchwords and the ideals of freedom, but they sound hollow and insincere because you know they can never be realized by the dictatorship you advocate or by any other means. Be content then to see your fellow-men as they are, and to foresee that they will degenerate unless you prevent it: concern yourselves as politicians with the one question—how can we save a little of our civilization from the collapse which threatens it, and renounce all allies whose ideal is either freedom or material prosperity? Do not count on progress or providence, or dialectical materialism to do your work for you, but recognize yourselves as a tiny company of individuals on whose actions the happiness of your country depends, and by whose philosophy the rightness of these actions is in turn determined.

"I read the other day a poem by one of your few great prophets and it seemed to express perfectly the spirit of your age and the problems you must face.

Turning and turning in the widening gyre
The falcon cannot hear the falconer;
Things fall apart: the centre cannot hold;
Mere anarchy is loosed upon the world,
The blood-dimmed tide is loosed, and everywhere
The ceremony of innocence is drowned;
The best lack all conviction, while the worst
Are full of passionate intensity.

Surely some revelation is at hand;
Surely the Second coming is at hand.
The Second Coming! Hardly are those words out
When a vast image out of *Spiritus Mundi*
Troubles my sight; somewhere in sands of the desert
A shape with lion body and the head of a man,
A gaze blank and pitiless as the sun,

Is moving its slow thighs, while all about it
Reel shadows of the indignant desert birds.
The darkness drops again; but now I know
That twenty centuries of stony sleep
Were vexed to nightmare by a rocking cradle,
And what rough beast, its hour come round at last,
Slouches towards Bethlehem to be born?[1]

I would advise you to consider this prophecy and, bearing it in mind, to give up your Utopias and your reckless belief in the common man. Judge Russia not by theory, but by fact, and study Stalin the ruler, not Marx the publicist. When you have done so, I am sure that you will resolve to impose on your country a dictatorship as severe and as permanent as the Russian, and to drive out the philosophy of materialism as ruthlessly as Stalin has banished the spirit of true philosophy and the belief in the immortal soul."

[1] W. B. Yeats, *Collected Poems*, pp. 210-11.

PLATO to his friend Aristotle, Greetings. Knowing, my dear Aristotle, your interest in the classification of constitutions, I have long intended to write to you concerning my journey back to the world of space and time and to relate my experiences to you. Now that occasion offers and I am returned to England, where I am at present a guest, I am anxious to pose you a problem which will tax even your genius for analysis and definition. For I have visited one of these modern nations called Germany and studied its new revolutionary government, and I am still puzzling myself to discover in which of my classifications I shall put National Socialism—this is the name they give both to their creed and to their constitution.

Let me, therefore, expound to you quite simply the problem which confronts me. And in order that this matter may be perfectly clear, you must excuse me if I narrate to you something which happened to me during my stay in the capital of Germany. For while I was there I attended a great assembly of the people. In one covered hall were gathered close on thirty thousand men and women—though you will be glad to hear the women took no part save to applaud and to look with pleasure on the uniforms and physique of the men. The gathering was well disciplined and gay with flags and uniforms and the public—unlike our own unruly Greek assemblies—applauded only at certain pre-arranged times, and then not with the confused hubbub of a democratic crowd, but with short and incisive shouts like the barking of well-trained dogs. At this I was well pleased, since they had clearly come not to criticize their leaders but to receive from them inspiration and hope.

There were many speakers, but two particularly attracted my notice. The first was a small lame man, whose face bore a strong resemblance to the Hittite type which we used sometimes to see in the Peiraeus. He was clearly a demagogue, not concerned with truth but with persuasion, and I therefore studied all that he said most carefully, being anxious to learn what sort of "noble lie" the National Socialists provide for their common people. But the second speaker was a philosopher, a learned man trained in academic research and professing to distinguish truth from rhetoric; and to him I also listened carefully in order to discover what is the philosophy of National Socialism, the esoteric truths of the faith which none but the elect can understand.

In order that you may appreciate my difficulty to the full, I will repeat to you—as well as I can remember it—something of what each speaker said. Do not convict me of falsehood if some details fall short of perfect accuracy, but rest assured that the general tenor is correct. After much else, which is not to the point, the little man who looked like a Hittite spoke as follows:

". . . for National Socialism springs from the German soul and boldly vindicates the German conception of race as the fundamental unity upon which the State must be based. It claims that the deep sense of community, which we Germans feel when we stand together on the field of battle, cannot be analysed into an ideological superstructure whose real basis is mercenary self-seeking. Only a people who have permitted their stock to be contaminated with the blood of colonial peoples can accept the individualist philosophy of life which founds the State upon the rationalistic contract of a gang of Jews. We Germans, thanks to a deep sense of blood-brotherhood which binds us together and which enables us to reject instinctively any 'citizen' of mongrel stock, know that the doctrines of Liberalism and Democracy and Marxism are all variants of one foul disease with which the Jews seek to infect our people, to weaken its strength and so to gain the upper hand. For we have seen how those conspirators rigged up the constitution of Weimar—with its mathematical 'equality,' its 'individual rights,' and its 'toleration'—with the express purpose of eradicating our true German tradition of obedience to leadership, self-sacrifice for the community and death for the traitor.

"For we must be clear in our minds, fellow-Germans, that the enemy is crafty and sly. Dividing his forces, he gives them different names and pretends they are opposed to one another. He does that to deceive you and to lull you into false security. In France he veils his filthy countenance under the form of democracy. In Russia he openly flaunts the Jewish ideal of class-hatred. But he cannot hoodwink us. World-capitalism and Communism are both internationalist organizations willing to sacrifice everything to swell their money-bags, and to suck the blood of women and children. Democracy is lined up on the side of Marxist dictatorship and the criminals of east and west are employing the League of Nations once more to encircle our country and to deny us our place in the sun.

"This world conspiracy against the German people is proved by the famous Protocol of the Elders of Zion. It does not affect my argument that this protocol is said to be a 'forgery': so-called scientific proof cannot contravert the fact that in that document the very essence of *Hebraic Reason* is disclosed. No scientist can disprove our racial theory since it does not consist of biological concepts but is the expression of the German philosophy of life. Racialism is not an international science but a German creed, and though ten thousand intellectuals disprove it, our own German blood will scorn their rational argumentation: we shall always KNOW deep down and instinctively who our enemy is. World Jewry does not simply mean the subhuman members of the Jewish species: world Jewry is the spirit of Jewish reason wherever it is found, the spirit of Jewish religion in every land, the octopus of class-war and capitalist cruelty which threatens to strangle the Aryan race, to dry up its life-blood and so to weaken our European culture that it succumbs to the menace of Oriental Bolshevism.

"It is this spirit of Jewish reason which in the last two hundred years has permeated European culture and well-nigh destroyed it. In capitalism it invented an economic machine to exploit the natural wealth of nations and to divide the spoils among the high-priests of world finance: a machine whose imperialism and rapacity mobilizes the masses to fight not for their countries but for the interests of world Jewry. In Christianity it found a religion of humility and brotherly love to sap the vitality of the race: so that Christian humanitarians now spend millions a year on preserving the unfit and the cripples and in encouraging them to breed at the cost of the healthy and strong. In Liberalism and Communism it found philosophies ready to make the nonsensical assertion that all men are equal and rational, to deny blood-brotherhood and the distinction of leader and follower and so to subject the Western world to the rule of the machine and of finance. In democracy it found a system of government calculated precisely to accentuate party differences, to put power into the hands of political bosses and to destroy the natural leadership of the nation. Jewish reason instigated the failure of democracy in order to introduce communism, and finally to enslave the German people to Jewish Bolshevism.

"But Jewish reason has not been content to befoul our politics. It has seeped into our universities and schools. Everywhere its destructive spirit of ridicule has tried to weaken our German spirit and to replace German culture and manners with the drab morality of an international cultural Bolshevism. Culture, my friends, springs from the organic life of the race. Cultural Bolshevism tries to kill that life by clamping on us all the machine-made products of the intellect. It destroys imagination and romance and replaces them with rationalistic cleverness.

"Everywhere you look, you will find the enemy. True to his loathsome nature, he knows the arts of concealment and subterfuge, of alias and alibi. You must smell him out and when you have found him I know that you will not be knock-kneed or snivel Christian sentimentalities, but will have your revolvers ready.

"But let us turn to the positive side of our task. National Socialism has triumphed: it has destroyed democracy and forestalled the Communist conspiracy within Germany itself. It has knocked on the head a few Socialists and Liberals and Pacifists and Democrats—incurable degenerates—and it has locked up the cases which were not so hopeless and given them a taste of German education. The German people has been freed from its slavery to an un-German creed, and, conscious of its destiny once more, is working as a blood-brotherhood for the Cause. The faction and dissension bred by parliamentary institutions has been suppressed: the doctrine of class-war has been eradicated from the German heart, and the employee and employer collaborate once more for the good of the nation. Only the Churches have been reluctant to toe the line, but, since we have the youth of the nation behind us, we can afford to disregard the snivelling scrupulosities of Lutheran greybeards and of the black moles. Germany has rekindled the flame of German tradition, and strong in that tradition we have smashed unemployment at home and the League of Nations abroad. The whole world trembles before us—or rather, the statesmen tremble—while the peoples become gradu-

ally aware of their Aryan inheritance and look to us
to liberate them from their miseries."

I was well pleased with this speech, displaying, as
it did, an understanding of the popular mind which
can only appreciate half-truths tricked up in the
vulgar trimmings of symbol and myth. For I need
not assure you that none of what he said approximated even to the truth, or that the Jewish people,
like all others, is composed of good and bad, stupid
and intelligent, and so on. But the speaker had seen
that the "noble lie" need not take account of scientifically ascertainable fact, but must always express truth
in the form of a symbol, and so, for reasons which I
need not go into, he had chosen the Jew to represent
all things evil and dangerous for the common man.
But most subtle of all, he had grasped that reason,
which for us is the highest good, is for the vulgar a
snare and a delusion, and therefore in his "noble
lie" he displayed an irony worthy of Socrates himself,
making reason and philosophy the chief cause of all
our troubles, and abusing the Jew for possessing the
most priceless treasure of man. How I relished the
impudence of the fellow, seeing well that he had
reason enough and to spare and had yoked it to the
service of the very rhetoric and "intellectualism"
which he so vehemently denounced. If he is strictly
subjected to the commands of a philosopher, I
thought, he can indeed be entrusted with the task of
controlling the popular passions. For he has the power
of uniting them in a common purpose, of making
them forget their present discomforts and pains for
the sake of future bliss, and of fixing in their minds

the picture of an enemy for whose destruction they will risk all. But since this enemy is only a *symbol* with no real counterpart, he can manipulate it and disguise it in countless garbs, so that anything which it is to the interest of the State to oppose and to destroy, appears to the people as an example of Jewish reason, and anything which is to be defended and advanced is seen as an instance of Aryan virtue. In this way, by the use of these two myths, he is able to raise up a well-nigh fanatical enthusiasm among the populace for any enterprise which he may undertake.

And I observed that the people were well pleased with the "noble lie." Buffeted and bruised by many years of war and political faction, uncertain of employment, and subjected to currency manipulation and commercial intrigues on whose ingenuity and devilments even our traders and bankers would gaze with amazement, they had grown weary of a self-government which was no self-government, but the tyranny of politicians and generals and industrialists. They had been filled, as all these modern democracies were, with vague religious ideals of brotherhood and love and understanding, and had believed that parliamentary government was somehow or other connected with these ideals. And so, when they were defeated in war, they set up a democratic regime and stretched out friendly arms to the democracies which had defeated them. Poor souls! They were speedily disillusioned. For the modern democracies are as nationalist and imperialist in their actual policy— whatever their sentiments may be—as the Athens of

Pericles and even of Cleon. After the war they set up a League of Nations which, like our own Delian League, degenerated into an empire, or rather, an instrument of empire, for control of which the Great Powers within it fiercely struggled—all the while speaking words as honeyed and as high-sounding as Pericles himself.

And so at last the common people in Germany were schooled by hard necessity to see that democracy is only agreeable for a people with money to spend and rich men to squeeze; and that though it is pleasant to allow open competition for shares in a large cake, it is not so pleasant to fight for a loaf of bread against rich and influential people. For they go off with the bread and the common man preserves only the freedom to starve.

This the German people saw with regard both to home and to foreign affairs. For in Germany itself, as the class-war grew fiercer, the plight of the common people became steadily worse: and abroad, the disturbances of trade caused by the Great War compelled the victorious democracies to regard Germany as a rival and not as a friend, and to seek by every means to prevent her jeopardizing their own trade.

Thus history was preparing the German people to accept a revolution and to welcome a dictatorship which should impose order upon their own troubled lives and should, by force of arms and by the rugged language of the soldier, expose the hypocrisies of the League of Nations. Now among the townsmen and the labourers in the factories there was a resolve to impose the dictatorship of the Communists, and this might well have been achieved if the leaders had not befuddled the minds of their followers with talk of self-government and workers' control and suchlike democratic foolery. For these leaders could never make up their minds whether they wished to be democratic demagogues or dictators, and so the people had no confidence in them—which was just as well—and turned with enthusiasm to the "noble lie" of the National Socialists. Within the space of a few months these remarkable men had conquered power, thanks to the financial aid which was rendered by the industrialists and to the rhetoric of leaders like the lame man whom I had just heard.

I have related all this to you so that you may appreciate to the full the capacities of the fellow. Rest assured he does not need to study your *Politics* in order to discover how to retain his power. And so let us leave him and turn our attention to the second speaker.

You can imagine with what eagerness I awaited his words. For I said to myself, "He must be no mean philosopher if he can control a sophist so cunning as this fellow has proved himself to be. But since he is a gentleman, well-bred and well-educated (as the first speaker was not), no doubt he has within him a soul more resolute and an intelligence more powerful than even my friend Dion in Syracuse." In this surmise I was to be sadly disappointed. For judge of my horror and amazement when he said:

"Fellow Germans, you have heard the wonderful speech of the Doctor, and you will agree with me that he has expressed the supreme truths of German

philosophy. I am an academic, and I freely admit to
you that, before the revolution, I did not actively
support National Socialism. I was blinded by the
Jewish Press and by my fellow academics—most of
whom, I am glad to say, are now in exile largely
owing to my zeal—and did not then see the divine
qualities of our leader or the place which God has
given him in German history. But now my eyes are
opened and I am content to serve as a humble col-
laborator in the great work of national regeneration.
I see now that intellect and criticism must be schooled
to accept the promptings of intuition and of that
knowledge which streams in the blood of the Aryan
and challenges the barren logic of Liberalism. I have
renounced that scientific spirit which is a product of
Jewish intellect and I am devoting my services to
the cause we all have at heart. Before the great days
of March 1933 I called myself a philosopher and pre-
tended to study Plato: but, in fact, I contented
myself with petty elucidation of the text and tried to
read into him my Liberal prejudices. I confess this
all to you openly, and I thank God that my students
burnt all the books which I then wrote. I have now
written a great work entitled *Platon und der Ursprung
des Nationalsozialistischen Staatsgedankens*. For it is my
intention to prove to the world that all that is true
in philosophy can be found, if you search long
enough, in the pages of *Mein Kampf*, and that for
this reason Plato, in so far as he spoke the truth, was
a prototype of National Socialism. In this book I
maintain that Plato preached the revolution which
Adolf Hitler has so wonderfully carried through,

the spiritual regeneration of his people from commercialism, individualism, and cultural Bolshevism. Rejecting the degenerate democracy of Athens, he turned to aristocratic Sparta and sought in Syracuse to rekindle the Spartan spirit. Sparta was a military State: and the Spartan citizen was a soldier of Laconia (as his land was called)—laconic in his speech as a soldier should be. From boyhood he lived a soldier's life and the State saw to his education. The boys were divided into 'packs' under the leadership of an elder boy and were given a Spartan training. Their food and their dress was simple: their intellectual education, that which a soldier needs. They went barefoot, and they were encouraged to steal if they were hungry: but they were flogged if the theft was discovered. For to learn to steal successfully teaches the art of ambush and forage which every warrior needs. This Spartan education is a wonderful prototype of our Aryan ideals. It subordinates the individual to the State, and the follower to the leader; and it develops those qualities of courage, simplicity, and discipline which are the marks of a warrior—and of a ruling race.

"Sparta was Plato's ideal, and it is our German ideal too. We, like Plato, reject the luxury and intrigue and intellectualism of Athens: we reject the imperialism which democracy brings; we reject the principle of mathematical equality which enables the demagogue and the commercial magnate to rob the natural ruler of his power. We too claim that the common people need not self-government but good government: and we believe that the statesman's job is the education of a warrior class to whom the protection of the people can be entrusted.

"But how was it that Plato the Athenian advocated in his *Republic* the restoration of the Spartan State? Because, my friends, Plato was greater than the Athens in which he lived. He was able to free himself from her corrupting influence and to recreate in his mind the vision of the true Greek city-state, a simple community of warrior-rulers and happy peasants, and he had the courage to tell his fellow-citizens that they must learn their lesson from Sparta. Of course in his writings there are still traces of the individualism and intellectualism of Athenian thought; but if we are to discover the true Plato we must disregard these blemishes and realize that Plato, in his early years, fell under the dangerous influence of Socrates, the prophet of sophistical rationalism, the sceptical defamer of the city-state. Plato was at first charmed by his cleverness, his verbal agility, and his apparent opposition to democracy, and for many years he succumbed to a dangerous intellectualism. But in the *Republic* his aristocratic spirit reasserted itself; he renounced Socrates and claimed kinship with Sparta; he discarded toleration and a weak sympathy with the common man and, aware of his spiritual vocation, advocated the concentration of all power in the hands of the bearers of Aryan culture—the warriors. The *Republic* is the abnegation by the pupil of a perverse master, and the assertion that even friendship must be sacrificed to the cause of the Aryan race; it is, indeed, the philosophical archetype of that terrible decision which our leader himself made on June 30, 1934."

You can imagine my feelings! Dionysius' book on my philosophy[1] was nothing to this. I was just about to rise to my feet when I noticed that the audience had already become exceedingly restive and that the chairman had hurriedly pushed the philosopher off the dais. I therefore made my way towards him, plucked him by the sleeve, and disguising my identity, said to him with all the self-control I could muster, "I should be obliged if you could speak to me for a moment." The philosopher recognized me for a foreigner by my accent and (hoping, I presume, to advance his position by persuading me of the excellence of all things German) immediately complied with my request.

I will not waste your time with the details of our conversation. Anxious to retain the sobriety which is the mark of the true philosopher, I did not at once attack him for his slanders on the memory of Socrates, but turned the talk to Sparta and politely expressed my interest at his delight with Spartan ideals. I asked him if he really thought that Germany was like Sparta, and when he replied affirmatively, I reminded him that in Sparta the Helot serfs outnumbered the Spartans by fifteen to one, and that for this reason the Spartiates, always in fear of revolt, organized a secret police to murder any Helot who showed any initiative. Did he think that on this point there was any resemblance? Not bothering to wait for a reply, I went on to show that Sparta was an agricultural community, that all wealth was forbidden to its ruling class, and that in this way the Spartans avoided

[1] See Plato, Letter VII, 341.

Q

the imperialism of Athens. With no interest in markets or raw materials and with a ban on the participation of the citizen in trade, they had no incentive to foreign adventures. Furthermore the terror of Helot revolts kept them always at home. Such was the condition of Sparta: did he press the analogy here? Did he suggest that in Germany capitalism had been suppressed or that the National Socialist was forbidden all access to wealth? Of course he did not. Germany was an industrial State with the same needs and aspirations as any democracy, and in Germany the industrialist has even more influence in politics than in the democracies.

I admit to you that all this was easy game, but I felt it my duty to expose to this professor of philosophy the full depths of his ignorance and turpitude and self-deception, and so I concluded the matter by saying, "My dear sir, there were among the Athenians many who admired Sparta, but none of us were blind to her failings. Plato most of all attacked the onesidedness of her education and the vile condition of her serfs. As for your suggestion that your new State has a Spartan constitution simply because it has adopted her boorishness and cruelty as an instrument for suppressing democracy and furthering its imperialist pretensions, that is fantastic, and you know it."

He agreed reluctantly, muttering something about not pressing analogies too far; but I would not let him go, and went on to discuss the *Republic*, showing that I, so far from renouncing Athens, had tried to fuse together the virtues of Athenian reason with

those of Spartan morale. I had tried to turn the
tyranny of a cruel militarism into the gentle rule of
the philosopher who is resolved to give happiness to
his people, and sacrifices the pleasures of wealth and
family to fit himself for the task of ruling. I argued
that I denounced militarism as fiercely as I denounced democracy, and that no one had praised
reason and intellect more highly than I. And then I
turned on him personally and said: "My friend—for
we must be friendly to all—you call yourself a
philosopher and you have been privileged to enjoy
all the advantages which money and education can
lavish on a man. You have chosen the highest calling
which man can choose and claim to have devoted
yourself to the service of truth and wisdom. And yet
you have dared to declare before your countrymen
that philosophy must serve the 'noble lie' and that
reason must be the instrument of intuition and of
the blood. You call yourself not only a philosopher,
but a patriot too; and yet you dare to besmirch the
name of Socrates who, above all men, strove to
harmonize these two vocations and died in the
attempt. I tell you that in so doing you have proved
yourself a coward, unworthy both of philosophy and
of your State. For what has happened? A great
revolution has taken place, and a chance has been
given to you in that shift of power to make the
influence of truth and philosophic integrity once
again supreme in Germany. The people are disciplined and content to obey the commands of the
soldiers and demagogues who have gained control.
And yet you professors and philosophers and

scientists, instead of seeing the duty which rests on your shoulders of gaining control over the new leaders, and imposing on their myths the law and order which would give them shape, have accepted these myths as truth, toadying to the men you should command, and intriguing against one another for comfortable positions in the new order. It was your duty to uphold the intellectualism of Athens, and to set it over the Spartan virtues of the military class: to see to it that the vested interests should not turn and twist the Aryan myth to their own advantage, making of your new discipline an instrument of selfish economic oppression. Above all, you should have retained your universities pure and intact from the noble lies which must be provided for the lower orders, and seen to it that there, at least, the spirit of pure research was preserved and strengthened by a resolution among you all to shrink at nothing in order to achieve power in the State.

"But instead of this you have flattered and pampered the new rulers, like lackeys fearful of losing their weekly wage. You have proclaimed as philosophic truths the myths and symbols of the politicians and have allowed your universities to become the home of vulgar propaganda and sophistical half-truths. You will tell me that it was impossible for you to gain power and influence, and that the new rulers were not amenable to reason. My good sir, that may possibly be true, but it is not a truth which *you* have tested. My two best friends gave their lives in the attempt. Socrates was executed by the Athenians, and Dion was murdered at Syracuse. They did not shrink from the uttermost danger to proclaim the cause of truth on every occasion and to persuade the rulers to see the error of their ways and to entrust the conduct of affairs to reason. They in their time were prepared to give their lives, but you and your associates will not risk your pay. Instead, you slyly prostitute the cause of truth to rhetoric and sophistry.

"I do not only refer to the members of your universities, but to all the 'educated' gentlemen who now sit passive under the tyranny of myth. I know that a few, inspired with true philosophy, have retired into private life or fled to exile so that the rest of the world may not forget that your country was once famous for its promotion of truth, and that Germans can still prefer philosophy to prosperity. But the majority are like yourself, and as a result the 'noble lie' which could be the means of happiness to all is become an instrument of insane destruction. Believed no less by the rulers than by their subjects, it has effected not regeneration, but tyranny. For the motives of your rulers are ambition and power. They have suppressed democracy only to replace it by intrigue and secret corruption and palace revolution.

"But this is not to be accounted to their fault. They are men who know no better, loyal and devoted when knowledge rules, but cruel and insensate when power is left to them alone. Long ago I foretold what would happen in such a State, and I cannot do better before I let you go then to repeat to you my own words:

" 'Such then will be the revolution. But after the revolution how will it be governed? . . . It will distrust the wise rulers, for its wise men will now be of mixed character, not simple and sincere as before; it will prefer spirited and more straightforward men, made more for war than for peace, will have a great admiration for military tricks and stratagems, and will always be engaging in war.

" '. . . These men will be avaricious . . . with a fierce secret passion for gold and silver. They will have storehouses and treasuries of their own where they will store their wealth in secret. They will be ringed round with dwellings, mere private nests where they may squander a lavish expenditure on their wives, and whomsoever they please.

" '. . . They will be sparing of their money . . . but their desires will make them enjoy spending other men's money. They will pluck the fruits of pleasure in secret, running away from the law, like boys running away from their father. Compulsion and not persuasion will have controlled their education, because they have neglected the true Muse, who is accompanied by reason and philosophy, and have honoured gymnastics above music.' "[1]

"You described," he said, "a constitution compounded throughout of good and evil."

"Yes, it is a compound," I said. "But one single feature is conspicuous in it, and that is rivalry and ambition."

When I had spoken thus, I bade him a curt farewell.

[1] See *Republic*, 547.

Such, my dear Aristotle, were my experiences in Germany, and I have related them at length, because I was sure it would interest you to see that human nature has not changed profoundly since you died. When I return I will ask you to give your opinion on my analysis of the German State, which I hold to be a mixed constitution containing elements of both timocracy and oligarchy, and also to chide me if I was too severe with the calumniator of my friend Socrates. For I remember that you were always calmer in your judgment and, expecting little of mankind, were less shocked by iniquity than I.

WE have tried in the preceding chapters to discover how Plato would have faced the problems of a world very different from his own. We have seen his criticism, and sometimes his ridicule of existing institutions, and we have discovered some concrete proposals which he would probably make. We have, in fact, staged the *Republic* in modern dress, and it is now for us to consider our own attitude to it and to ask ourselves whether we are convinced by the Platonic analysis and the Platonic solution of our problems.

Before we do so, however, it may be wise to discover how Plato fared in his own Greek world, and how his theories worked out when applied in his own day—to resume, in fact, the story of his life which we broke off in the middle of Chapter 5. There we had reached the moment when in 367 he set sail for Sicily, resolved to turn a king into a philosopher. Syracuse, where young Dionysius II ruled, was at this time the largest city in the Western world; three times as big as Athens and the Peiraeus put together. It was the capital of the Sicilian Greeks and the bulwark of Hellenism against Carthage. The menace of Carthage had been for the Western Greeks the dominating fact of foreign politics. In the same year (480) that Athens defeated Persia, Syracuse, under the military dictatorship of Gelon, had defeated Carthage and ensured the independence of the Greek cities for half a century. From 480 to

420 they too had prospered: Sicily and South Italy had become one of the granaries of the world and the centre of considerable industrial activity too. Then in 415 had come the attempt by Athens to include Sicily in her Empire, successfully repelled by Syracuse. But throughout their history the Western Greeks were like their Aegean kinsmen. Only danger could unite them; when that was passed they quarrelled with each other, and Sicily and South Italy were in a state of intermittent warfare. Prosperity here, as in the Aegean, brought class-war; democrats and oligarchs struggled for power in each town and wasted their strength in a war of attrition. It is not surprising therefore that, when in 409 Carthage launched a new attack on Sicily, the Greeks fell an easy prey to a disciplined military power. In 406 Agrigentum was sacked and its lovely temples ruined: in 405 even Syracuse was threatened. Once more, as in 480, only one thing could save Hellenism in the west—military dictatorship to put down dissension, to instil order and to build up a united front against Carthage. In 405 Dionysius I, a young soldier of twenty-five, seized power in Syracuse. With the help of a highly paid bodyguard and foreign mercenaries he smashed the political factions, gained the support of the people, and set himself up as democratic dictator. Democracy voted itself out of any but a formal existence.

Dionysius was a remarkable man, a living example of the *Realpolitiker* whom Plato portrayed in the character of Callicles.[1] Power was the only force

[1] See page 79.

which he recognized in politics; tradition, liberty, and aristocracy were for him outworn things. Syracuse must become the centre of the anti-Carthaginian movement and the international anarchy be crushed. He therefore defeated and destroyed many of the independent Greek cities and moved their populations to new Syracuse, planting in their stead loyal colonies of soldiers. Money was needed for armaments; he therefore taxed mercilessly, stripped the temples, and scrupled at no means of collecting wealth. Men were needed to fight; he therefore freed slaves and serfs, smashed the aristocratic re-action, and hammered the Syracusan proletariat into some sort of unity. Hated by aristocrat, industrialist, moralist, and workman alike, abused by historians and philosophers as a foul and bloody tyrant, he yet succeeded in forging a war machine with which for thirty years he kept Carthage at bay, and at last made a peace by which two-thirds of the island remained in his possession.

Such was the man whom Plato visited on his first voyage to Sicily in 388 B.C. The philosopher was deeply shocked by all he saw; the ruthless tyranny and the luxurious life of the court alike disgusted him, and he was bold enough to say so. Dionysius, in fury, inquired what his business might be in Sicily, to which Plato replied that he came to seek a virtuous man. "Waste of time," said the tyrant shortly, and the interview closed. But Plato could never forget the morose grandeur of the soldier who trusted no friend, lived in terror of assassination and yet had saved Greek independence. Condemning him as he did, he could not deny his achievements, or the brute fact that force had prevailed to achieve a unity which no gentlemanly discussion of scruples had achieved.[1]

Moreover, Dion, Plato's favourite pupil, was an influential figure at the court; his sister was one of Dionysius' wives, his father had been one of his best generals, and he himself was a trusted negotiator and a good soldier. Through Dion therefore Plato could exert a decisive influence on the largest city in the world, the strongest military defender of Greek independence. When in 367 the old tyrant died, Dion had hoped to gain some share of power for his own nephew, but Dionysius II, son of Dionysius' foreign wife, was too quick for him and seized the throne. Dion, however, remained the most powerful individual in the court and, in spite of the opposition of Philistus, an able general and his rival for power, persuaded the young man to invite the famous philosopher as his adviser. Dionysius was a shrewd but inexperienced youth, a dilettante by nature, and he was tickled by the idea. It seemed possible that under Plato's influence he might develop into a true philosopher-king: at least it was clear that here, if anywhere, was an opportunity to test the practicality of Plato's political plans.

It is essential to discover the nature of Plato's intentions when he sailed for Syracuse in 367. Fortunately, in the letters which he wrote long afterwards, he has given us some indications. In the first place, he was resolved to withdraw Dionysius from

[1] See *Republic*, 566 ff., for a description.

the corrupting influence of the court, imbue him with the moral ideals of the Academy, and put him through the course of mathematical and philosophical study which he held to be the necessary basis of statesmanship. Only if the tyrant became a philosopher could the rest of the policy be carried through. Secondly, he was resolved to relax the iron discipline of the military dictatorship which Dionysius I had exercised over the Sicilian Greeks. Force must only be used to impose justice, and the philosopher-king must turn his attention to the education of his countrymen, and to purging the court of its luxury and self-indulgence. A voluntary abnegation of wealth must be demanded of it, and a new ruling *élite* must be developed drawn from the aristocratic families and devoted to the cause of law and order. Thirdly, the Greek cities of Sicily, destroyed by Dionysius, must be rebuilt on the basis of aristocratic institutions, and set under the constitutional monarchy of the young philosopher-king.

It is probable that at this period the Platonic programme comprised no more than these three points, since Plato believed that once the new philosopher-kings were in power, everything else would follow of its own accord. The new cult was welcomed by Dionysius and philosophy became a royal craze. Plutarch has given us a picture of this strange phenomenon.

"This was the state of affairs when Plato came to Sicily, who, at his first arrival, was received with wonderful demonstrations of kindness and respect. For one of the royal chariots, richly ornamented, was in attendance to receive him when he came on shore; Dionysius himself sacrificed to the gods in thankful acknowledgment for the great happiness which had befallen his government. The citizens also began to entertain marvellous hopes of a speedy reformation when they observed the modesty which now ruled in the banquets and the general decorum which prevailed in all the court, their tyrant himself also behaving with gentleness and humanity in all the matters of business that came before him. There was a general passion for reasoning and philosophy, insomuch that the very palace, it is reported, was filled with dust by the concourse of the students in mathematics who were working out their problems there. Some few days later, it was the time of one of the Syracusan sacrifices; and when the priest, as he was wont, prayed for the long and safe continuance of the tyranny, Dionysius, it is said, as he stood by, cried out, 'Leave off praying for evil upon us.' This sensibly vexed Philistus and his party, who conjectured that if Plato, upon such brief acquaintance, had so far transformed and altered the young man's mind, longer converse and greater intimacy would give him such influence and authority that it would be impossible to withstand him."

The new policy was bound to raise dismay among Dion's rivals. Philistus was now banished, and it was suspected that the invitation to Plato was a device to ensure Dion's position at court. The tactlessness and self-righteous demeanour of Dion did nothing to dispel the suspicion. The devotee of the ideals of the Academy was something of a prig, and his puritanism had a ruthless flavour to it which suggested that ambition and self-interest were mixed with its idealism. Dion at least showed no signs of surrendering his palatial house and princely income, or of sacrificing the pleasures of wealth for pure philosophy. But there were more serious critics, who urged that the reformers were undoing the achievements of Dionysius I. Sicilian unity had been achieved and maintained by force of arms, and by the support of the commercial interests. To relax the dictatorship, to oust industry from political control, and to entrust power to callow idealists, would break the unity achieved at such terrific cost. Hastily Philistus, the hard-headed politician of the old school, was recalled, and began to suggest to the young tyrant the dark motives which Dion's idealism might cloak. Meanwhile Dionysius' enthusiasm for mathematics had cooled and he began to ask why he should pursue these weary studies before beginning the more practical—and glorious—work of reform. Plato's austerity impressed but also annoyed him, and his high moral tone began to jar. On the other hand, the eyes of the Greek world were upon him: if he dismissed Plato, it would be said that the great philosopher had found him unworthy. He decided on a compromise, banished Dion from Sicily, and retained Plato in courteous captivity. A month or two later a minor war broke out. Dionysius had no more time for philosophy and bade his friend a polite "good-bye," extracting a promise from him to return soon, and on the way home to negotiate an alliance between Syracuse and Plato's friend, Archytas

the Pythagorean ruler of Tarentum. Thus the honour
of both was saved and Plato within a year was back
in Athens, having apparently converted the greatest
tyrant in Greece to his philosophy.

It is possible that Plato might never have returned
to Syracuse had it not been for Dion's private affairs.
Dionysius, apprehensive that the latter might use his
wealth for counter-revolutionary purposes, con-
fiscated all that Dion had left in Sicily, and to test
whether he had given up all hope of return, suggested that he should allow his wife (whom he had
left behind) to be married to another courtier. Dion
indignantly refused, whereupon Dionysius began to
sell up his estate and, anxious to cause a rift between
his rival and the philosopher, invited Plato to resume
his position as adviser at Syracuse. Plato refused,
whereon Dionysius, with a polite suggestion of black-
mail, hinted that he would only hand over Dion's
property if Plato came. The philosopher hesitated,
but a letter from Archytas of Tarentum suggesting
that Syracuse might break off diplomatic relations if
he refused, tipped the scale in favour of another
attempt. In 361 he reluctantly returned to Sicily.

It seems probable that Dionysius was really intri-
gued by Plato's philosophy and anxious to discuss it
with him. But Plato would not allow the noblest of
human activities to become the hobby of a tyrant,
and sternly demanded that Dionysius should submit
himself to the full rigours of the Academic discipline.
Dionysius refused, but neither he nor Plato (for the
sake of their reputations) could allow the breach to
become public knowledge, and so Plato lived on in

the acropolis month after month while Dionysius
sold up the rest of Dion's estate and disposed of his
wife. The court and the mercenaries, deceived by
the official atmosphere of cordiality, began to suspect
Plato of undue influence, and he was nearly killed
during a mutiny of soldiers demanding higher pay.
At last Archytas sent a ship to rescue him and Plato
escaped.

Left to himself, Dionysius continued his philosophical studies, and tried to carry out the Platonic
programme, founding new cities and giving them
aristocratic constitutions on Plato's lines. Idealist
dilettantism began to weaken the structure of the
military dictatorship and it was clear that soon
Sicily would again become a prey to Carthaginian
invasion. But Dion had made up his mind. Meeting
Plato on his return, he informed him that he had
decided to conquer Syracuse and himself to impose
the rule of the philosopher-kings. Would Plato help?

His experiences in Sicily had broken Plato's spirit.
He was close on seventy and the enthusiasm which
had inspired the writing of the *Republic* had faded.
With it had gone the moral certitude which had justified him in his assertion that truth and right should
impose themselves by force. Syracusan politics had given
him a distaste for bloodshed and made him wonder
if any man were good enough to undertake the
responsibilities of absolute dictatorship. He began to
ask himself if the freedom and liberty of the subject
which he had so fiercely derided were, after all, so
futile. At least they gave some protection against
tyranny.

At the breath of these doubts, the Platonic plan for the salvation of Greece collapsed like a pack of cards. Plato had denounced all constitutional government and advocated the dictatorship of the good. His disdain for legal forms and the details of legislation had been based on a conviction that the education of the rulers could replace them. Now that he doubted if such rulers could be produced by his Academy, and began to pin his faith to detailed legislation as a check on absolutism, the political programme of the *Republic* became a Utopian dream. When Dion begged Plato to go with him, the philosopher refused, excusing himself on the grounds of old age and friendship with Dionysius, and remarking sagely that it is better to suffer injustice than to practise it.

But the younger members of the Academy were not of the same temper. For them the *Republic* was still a gospel and Dion the man to realize it. While Plato began sadly to work out a constitution and legislative programme for the new State, Dion was recruiting among his pupils. In 357, with a select staff of philosophers and five hundred men, he set sail to conquer the greatest city in Greece. The second attempt to put the dictatorship of the good into practice had begun—but the creator of the plan refused to participate. Instead, with anxious forebodings and a sense of future catastrophe, Plato said good-bye to the man he loved more than any other, and then returned to teach in an Academy emptied of many of its finest students.

The story of Dion's exploits in Sicily is a con-

fusion of romance, intrigue, disillusion, and murder.
The philosophers with just five hundred men turned
out Dionysius, captured Syracuse, and began once
more the attempt to build up a State in which there
should be neither military dictatorship nor yet a
democracy, but an authoritarian constitutional government. The experiences of the last ten years had
modified Dion's enthusiasm for the tyranny of
reason, and he now planned a constitution in which
the powers of the king should be largely formal;
while legislative, judicial, and executive control
should be centred in an elected committee of elder
statesmen. The forms of democracy were also to be
preserved in the meetings of the Assembly and of
the Council,[1] so that the new constitution was really
an attempt to work out a modern system of cabinet
responsibility to a popular assembly, and depended
(as modern democracy depends) for its success on a
social tradition strong enough to enable the cabinet
to exert real authority while listening to the wishes
of the people. If the cabinet failed to win the people's
confidence, then it would be forced to introduce an
open dictatorship: if, on the other hand, it abused
its position and showed no respect for the constitution, it had power enough to do so with impunity.

Dion's ideas pleased no one. The advocates of
unity and military strength for the war against
Carthage saw the reforms as a weakening of central
control. The democrats, observing that the committee of thirty-five was composed of wealthy men
and that all measures for the redistribution of wealth

[1] See page 141.

were rejected, concluded that this was merely another form of polite oligarchy; and one of Dion's colleagues—Heracleides—became the leader of a popular movement for the redistribution of the land. Civil war broke out; Dion was forced to rely on his foreign soldiers to quell the disturbances and was finally expelled by the democrats. After a period of confusion, however, he regained control and patched up a truce with Heracleides. But it soon became clear that if the democratic party were to be suppressed, open dictatorship was unavoidable. Heracleides was again at the head of the opposition, and Dion reluctantly gave his consent to the murder of his colleague.

The murder of Heracleides marks the end of the attempt to put Plato's philosophy into practice. The idealists had been forced by the pressure of necessity to behave no better and no worse than the old *Realpolitiker* whose regime they had denounced: the *Republic* had proved to be not an ideal constitution, but another variant of oligarchy, unwanted by the people, and as little relying on constitutional action or justice as naked tyranny. Dion was now a common murderer, living the selfsame life of fear and apprehension which he had seen in the courts of the older Dionysius, and suppressing with the selfsame ruthlessness all popular movements. In 353 Kallippus, one-time member of the Academy, and trusted minister at Dion's court, put himself at the head of a democratic conspiracy and, breaking into a dinner-party at Dion's palace, murdered his chief in cold blood.

It is probable that the shock for Plato was not
very great. The mission of the Academy to save
Sicily had ended in vulgar intrigue and butchery,
and the young men whom he had trained had proved
no better than their contemporaries unversed in true
philosophy. The republic, which Plato had resolved
to build so perfectly that even Socrates, the conscientious objector, could live there with a good
conscience, had proved itself no better than any other
oligarchy, and worse than the democratic Athens
which he had ridiculed and despised. All this was
true, but Plato had seen it long before Dion's death,
and had waited only for the inevitable conclusion.
The blood of Dion was on his head: he had inspired
him and sent him to his death, and he had taught
and approved his actual murderer. The application of
philosophy to practical life had failed, and Socrates'
death was still unatoned for by his disciple. Plato had
made it his life's mission to answer the question
Socrates asked and to find the justice which he
sought: he had not answered it, and instead of establishing justice he had instigated bloodshed and civil
strife.

Plato was seventy-five when he heard the news of
Dion's death. In his latter years he had turned more
and more to pure philosophical speculation and given
to the Academy that academic stamp which it was
to bear for the thousand years of its life and to impress on all future universities. He no longer despised
politics as vulgar and ridiculous: he feared them as
the terrible contaminator of pure and holy lives,
and tried to forget his own pangs of conscience in

contemplation of eternal reality. "It is better to suffer injustice than to practise it," and goodness, he now saw, could only be achieved by a complete renunciation of worldly power. If just government could not be attained by peaceful means, then it was better left unattempted: for the philosopher who puts his hand to bloodshed defiles his own soul and his own philosophy. In the last years of his life Plato was a pacifist.

But appeals still came from Dion's friends in Sicily, and all over the Greek world the rumour of the failure of the Academy was rife. Plato could not renounce politics even now and, summoning together all his failing strength, he composed two open letters to his former pupils in Sicily, at once advising them on future policy and defending himself against the charge that he was responsible for the catastrophe at Syracuse.

These letters are among the most pathetic historical documents which we possess. Rambling and discursive in style, they are the work of an old and broken spirit which feebly takes up one defence only to throw it away in disgust and pick up another, and, seeing that the main charge is irrefutable, seeks to divert attention to points of detail. Now he tries to persuade himself that Kallippos was not a real friend of Dion's, and that for this reason the murder was not so reprehensible: now suddenly, in the middle of narrating his own experiences in Syracuse, he launches into a bitter attack on Dionysius for publishing a book which purported to be an account of Platonic philosophy, and goes on to concentrate in three or four pages a brilliant summary of his views on the relations between language, thought, and reality. But always in the end he returns to his main theme, the salvation of Greek city-life and the cure of international and domestic anarchy which must be found if Carthage is to be beaten back; and feebly suggests to a Sicily, marred once more by a civil war, that unless men seek justice and obey law, no true happiness is available—cold comfort for men struggling for their lives, who realized too late that it was easier to break down the unity which military dictatorship had given than to replace it with the rule of law; and who, remembering the Academy, held Plato responsible not only for the murder of Dion but also for the inevitable victory of barbarian powers which time must bring.

In 347, at the age of eighty-one, Plato died. Ten years later the Macedonians conquered Greece; the age of Greek independence ended and the Alexandrian epoch began.

At the end of his life Plato knew that he had failed. Despite his eminence as a philosopher, he had not achieved the one thing on which he had set his heart. His researches in logic, in astronomy, and in mathematics could satisfy his thirst for knowledge and ensure him lasting fame: they could not console him for his failure to solve the problem which Socrates had set. For it was precisely the application of theory to practice, and of philosophy to everyday life, which Socrates had demanded and for which he had died. Plato had suppressed his natural inclination to wash his hands of politics because he felt himselr to be Socrates' disciple; he had dedicated the Academy to the memory of Socrates; and the failure of the Academy to win its way to the control of the city-state meant that Socrates' death was still unatoned. The spirit of disinterested criticism and scientific inquiry seemed to have contributed nothing to the elimination of social evils. It had diagnosed the disease, but the cure which it applied had been completely ineffective.

But does this mean that wisdom and reason can never be of practical use to the community? If so, the Academy must and should remain Academic, the cloistered refuge of the few who prefer truth to the other pleasures of life: and the politician, the banker, and the craftsman must and should reject the advice of the philosopher as useless or positively harmful.

If we do not accept this conclusion, then we must admit that Plato failed, not because he was a philosopher, but because there was something wrong with the methods which he employed and the plan upon which he worked; and it becomes of vital importance to discover these flaws in the programme of the *Republic*. For by discovering these, we shall be able to base our own political theory upon sound principles and to avoid the catastrophe which overwhelmed the Platonic statesmen.

In this chapter, then, I shall try to suggest some of the chief defects in Plato's theory and to show their relevance to our modern problems. Plato has criticized us: now it is for us in our turn to criticize him.

When we examine a great philosophical system it is the very simplest axioms which are most easily attacked, and the most "obvious" propositions which can most usefully be questioned. One such axiom of Plato's thought—and it is the justification of the whole political structure of the *Republic*—is that the common man is unreasonable. Let us start by a consideration of this assumption. Of course it is partly true. Human beings *are* often short-sighted, sentimental, and greedy, and if Plato had gone no further than this, he could not be gainsaid. But Plato assumed (1) that most men are naturally so deficient that they are incapable of self-government; (2) that there do exist potential rulers of such supreme wisdom that absolute government can be safely entrusted to them; and (3) that these potential rulers will mostly be found not among the peasants and artisans, but in the ranks of the gentry. Disregarding (3)—clearly the most questionable—we must admit that the first two propositions are clearly true. Mankind *is* stupid and from time to time men *do* arise so pre-eminent in virtue that power could be entrusted to them. But it does not follow that we can build the State on this assumption. "Statesmanship is the art of the second best": it takes men as it finds them, and it cannot presume that the man of genius will always be to hand. If we could rely upon a constant supply of supremely wise statesmen, we could disregard all questions of constitutional forms and political organization. It is precisely because we cannot do this that the problem of government is all-important. Thus though Plato's two propositions are true, they are

irrelevant to politics because the class of "wise men"
is not large enough or compact enough to become a
permanent ruling *élite* in any city or nation-state.

When, however, we add the third proposition, we
reach a conclusion which is not only irrelevant but
frankly partisan. The presumption that wise men
are not often found among the "working classes"
transforms the Republic from an ideal aristocracy in
the literal sense—the rule of the best—to an aristocracy of *birth*. The academic proposition, "the
best should rule," becomes a practical proposition,
"the best of the existing aristocracy should become
dictators" and the Platonic classes of rulers and
civilians merge into the Greek political factions of
aristocrats and democrats.[1]

Plato could defend this suggestion as sound
practical politics: he could say that in his opinion
and from his experience "the people" had thrown
up few leaders and that the aristocracy still retained
its traditions of public service. But in so doing he
surrendered his claim to base the *Republic* on philosophical principles and self-evident axioms: he
spoke no longer as a philosopher but as a citizen
and his judgment can properly be questioned by

[1] This point deserves fuller treatment than I can give it here.
Plato does in *Republic* 415 admit the bare possibility that a
'civilian' might be found worthy of promotion to the ruling
élite. This admission occurs, however, in a parenthesis and is no-
where elaborated. Since the education of the ruler begins at
birth, it is difficult to see how a craftsman could ever show
himself worthy of promotion. Plato, with his beliefs about
the degrading effects of 'banausic' occupations, can hardly have
considered it likely that he ever would.

anyone else with political experience. For he was advocating the claims of a certain social class—the dictatorship not of the best, but of the best members of the aristocracy—and assuming the latter to be identical with the former.

Thus there are two objections to Plato's argument. In the first place there will never be a sufficient number of pre-eminent men to form a ruling class in whom we can have complete confidence; and even if there were, it would be impossible to select them from the citizen population and to ensure that they alone should have political control. Plato himself often admitted this. He confessed that "good men" are corrupted by power, and he had seen enough of politics to know that irresponsible dictatorships—however carefully the dictators are selected and trained—always ends in disaster. And yet he advocated dictatorship!

In the second place his bias in favour of aristocracy led him to identify the "gentleman" with the good man, and he therefore, in searching for his *élite*, excluded the vast majority of the population from any serious examination. From the proposition "most men are incompetent to govern themselves," he glided imperceptibly into the assertion, "the working classes are incompetent to govern themselves."

The *Republic* is therefore a solution of the problem of government which could only be successful if men were not what they, in fact, are. Granting to the aristocratic *élite* absolute freedom of action, it demands of them a virtue far beyond their reach: demanding of the lower orders absolute obedience, it denies to them any possibility of self-realization. It makes the former divinity incarnate, the latter humanity with only a tiny spark of the divine. For this reason it is no surprise to discover the Platonic ideal realized in the structure of the Catholic Church. Substitute the clergy for the philosopher-kings, and the laity for the civilians, and you have the one practical fulfilment of the Platonic programme. But in the field of government, Platonism, because it is at once too ideal and not ideal enough, becomes the rational apologia for reaction. A military despot in Greece, a Roman emperor, a medieval monarch, a Renaissance prince or a modern dictator, and even a modern Conservative in a democratic State, can all justify themselves as Platonists, claiming special and providential wisdom for themselves and their friends, special and providential stupidity for the masses. Power will always vest itself in priestly robes to hide the wickedness of tyranny.

Thus although he denounced military despotism and aristocratic dictatorship, Plato was the aider and abettor of both, and tacitly countenanced them as the lesser of two evils. Confronted with the class-war, he dreamt that between the dictatorship of the Left and the dictatorship of the Right there was a third revolutionary alternative—the dictatorship of the "virtuous Right." But when we translate this dream into the sober language of politics, it is seen to be an empty illusion. For it advocates the formation of a party of good aristocrats opposed equally to the demands of rich and of poor, and the capture by this party of absolute political power. But since the membership of the party will be drawn almost exclusively from the antidemocratic side, it will be suspect to the working classes: and since it is opposed to the interests of the rich, it will be hated by them as well. Its government therefore will have no basis of consent and will be forced either to become a military dictatorship, or to concede to one side in the class struggle. Since it is resolutely antidemocratic, and is tied by bonds of kinship and tradition to the parties of the Right, there can be no doubt of the nature of those concessions. Resolved to suppress the equalitarian aspirations of the masses, it will rely on the support of the wealthy. In that case, it will find it impossible to destroy property and privilege as well. The "dictatorship of the virtuous Right" is transformed into a polite form of Fascism.

Plato had envisaged his "third alternative" as the creation of an impartial State, allotting to each man the life and work which he deserves, favouring no section of the community at the expense of others and harmonizing all interests for the common good. His ruling class was to be exalted above the clash of interests and, from the lofty heights of dictatorial power, to dispense justice objectively and dispassionately. This sublime vision neglected two simple facts. (1) No Government is absolutely supreme: for the power of the Government resides not only in the army and the civil service—its executive organs—but in those sections of the community which tolerate or support it. Where there is inequality of wealth and class-war—as there was in Greece—an absolute Government must be not only the master of all, but the servant of some. On seizing power the philosopher-kings must come to terms either with the rich or with the poor, in order to retain control. (2) Whatever the education provided by the Academy, the deep-seated instincts and traditions of the Greek aristocracy, its hatred and fear of pro-letarian dictatorship, and its exclusive sense of poli-tical status would combine to destroy the impar-tiality of the Platonic *élite*. We have seen in the history of Syracuse a terrible instance of these forces at work. By neglecting them, Plato had encouraged Dion to undertake a revolutionary *putsch* which could only end in disaster.

When Plato and Dion saw the impossibility of their philosopher-kings, they at last realized that the escape from class-dictatorship is not another dictator-ship but the denial of absolute power to anyone. The impartial State cannot be constructed from above by any ruling *élite*, vested with dictatorial authority, and resolute to harmonize conflicting interests. It must be the product of the harmony of those interests themselves. Only by the limitation of powers, and by the representation of all interests, is it possible to achieve justice and security. Impartiality and the rule of law are possible only if sovereignty is denied to any section or group whatsoever and re-placed by constitutional government. This new third alternative was dimly envisaged by Plato and Dion at the end of their lives. It implied the surrender of the whole programme of the Republic and of the Academy, but it substituted for them an equally fantastic plan.

For the transformation of the class struggle into
party warfare, of absolutism into constitutional
government, and of power politics into the rule of
law can only be effected where there is a pervasive
sense of national unity, a long-standing tradition on
the side of peaceful change and an expanding system
of production to supply the wealth needed for social
reform. These conditions were present in nineteenth-
century England: they were not present in fourth-
century Greece. The city-states had no sense of
national cohesion. The revolutionary upheavals of
the previous hundred years made any genuine co-
operation of rich and poor impossible. The steady
increase of slave-labour intensified the democratic
cry for a capital levy, distribution of land, and an
increase of "bread and circuses" for the citizen
population. And lastly, the menace of Macedonia in
the north and Carthage in the west necessitated
military dictatorship if Greek independence was to
be preserved. In these conditions the Platonic plan
for constitutional monarchy could please no one. It
was suspected by the democrats as a veiled form
of reaction, by the wealthy as a concession to the
lower orders, and by the patriot who cared more
for Greek independence than for domestic justice
as a dangerous weakening of that military discipline which was all-important for his ends. Plato's
second plan for the salvation of Greece failed as
signally as the first had failed, since it too tried to
construct an impartial state at a time when impartiality and "justice" were sheerly impossible, and
constitutional government was bound to become the

instrument of the Right in its struggle to suppress democracy.

This is perhaps the most valuable lesson which a study of Plato's life can teach us. The rule of law which allots to each man his due is a dream which can be realized only under certain specific conditions. It is the one thing which a revolutionary Government can never achieve, whatever its ideals. A revolution is always the resultant of a gross social maladjustment: and any Government which captures power after a revolution must suppress one side or the other. Only when society has adjusted itself to the new equilibrium of forces can those conditions of peaceful change arise which are essential both to constitutional government and to the impartial State. You cannot impose the rule of law or constitutionalism by peaceful discussion upon an economic and social anarchy, and if you try to do so you will merely be giving to one faction a spurious justification for its dictatorship. On the other hand, granted that a country has the supreme good fortune of achieving the economic and social equilibrium which permits of these things, it cannot retain them as realities unless the social and economic equilibrium is also maintained. If the system of production and distribution breaks down, no good will or idealism will prevent the destruction of social justice and the conversion of legality and constitutionalism into the instruments of power-politics. The third alternative once more disappears and decent men and women must once again make their choice between rival dictatorships and competing interests.

So far we have analysed Plato's conception of the "dictatorship of the good" and the "rule of law," and we have tried to show on the one hand that they were unrealizable in the Greek State, and on the other that they were twisted by Plato's aristocratic bias into justifications for counter-revolution. But this aristocratic bias had still more detrimental effects on Plato's political outlook. For he not only assumed that political leadership could only be found among the aristocracy, but also that all sound political ideals must be based upon the aristocratic and conservative tradition. We have seen how he neglected altogether the problem of slavery, and how he presupposed the autonomy of the city-state. We must now observe how he tried to restore the glories of Greece by returning to a well-nigh feudal economic and social order. The republic was to be divided into a Homeric order of warrior-kings, and a Homeric *demos* of craftsmen and peasants. It was to be economically self-sufficient, and to export only its surplus produce. Great disparities of income were to be avoided, and wealth was to be regulated according to need. Its noble rulers were, in fact, to be Spartan citizens softened by Athenian culture: its civilians, Spartan serfs raised to a higher level by the justice of a benevolent aristocracy. Plato conceived this social order as the true ideal of the Greek city-state, purged of the accretions which imperialism and commercialism had plastered over it; and in the *Republic* he tried to strip off the excrescences and display the perfect archetype of the Greek community. For this archetype he went far back to the days before the age of tyranny and the growth of trade, and claimed that agricultural aristocracy was the "true" form of Greek life. Big business, political parties, atheism, working-class unrest—these seemed to Plato blatant evils which must be abolished, and to abolish them he tried to revert to the period before they had arisen.

In so doing he neglected to observe that if they were evils, they were evils essential to the virtues of Greek civilization. The culture and the artistic glories of Athens would have been impossible without her commerce or her empire. Plato's own philosophical speculations were part and parcel of the rationalism which had destroyed the old religion and aristocratic authority. The independence of mind which caused working-class unrest had also made Socrates the first conscientious objector. To abolish these social evils by reverting to feudal aristocracy was to abolish also the glories of Greek life. In the second place the evils which Plato denounced were facts which could not be wished away. Slavery could not be made to vanish by neglecting its existence. The will to freedom and self-government among the craftsmen and peasants had been strong enough to sweep away aristocracy: it would not disappear because Plato announced its futility. The old religion and morality had perished: they could not gain new life by artificial respiration applied by a few philosophers. The romantic dream of resurrecting the golden age was bound to fail because the social and economic basis of that golden age had gone for ever.

Moreover, Plato's description of pre-industrial

S

Greece was largely mythical. Himself an individualist, a product of Athenian civilization, he interpreted history in terms of the present, and read into the past the fulfilment of his present wishes. Like the German romantics of the early nineteenth century, he first of all imagined an ideal State, then located it in the past, and then called on his countrymen to return to their true national traditions. Had he really studied history he might have seen that his Athenian ideas of education and culture could not be grafted on to the primitive stock, and that his ideal rulers—self-conscious and sophisticated Athenians, robed in mythological dress—were the products of the very commercialism which he denounced.

Through all Plato's work there runs this cult of pseudo-history. It makes much of the *Republic* a stiff and self-conscious pastiche, just as it made Dion, who felt himself to be a Platonic statesman, a consciously superior person. It is the cause of Plato's obsession that change is dangerous and that at all costs innovations, even in song and dance and literature, must be suppressed. Early Sparta was alive, but the new "Athenian Sparta" of Plato's dreams was a rigid and pedantic reconstruction of the past, dead because it could not face that dying of the old and growing of the new which is the essence of life. Just as Plato the poet denied himself poetry and let his imagination wither, so the *Republic* denies itself life, and takes on the stony look of a "classical" statue, the product of a tired civilization which rejects with senile agitation the vigour of youth and change.

Plato was a true reflection of one aspect of his

epoch: he embodied the ideals of a dying system. Beyond that system he could not look, and he had no eye for the seeds of the new order which was to replace it. And so the *Republic* is rooted in the past and is at bottom the rationalization and justification of Reaction. It is not—as is often supposed—typically Greek, or even typically Athenian: but the unique product of an Athenian aristocratic mind which tried to make sense out of the prejudices of its class, and succeeded in canalizing the activities of its best members into the preservation of a lost cause.

But even admitting all these criticisms, I still find the *Republic* the greatest book on political philosophy which I have read. The more I read it, the more I hate it: and yet I cannot help returning to it time after time. For it *is* philosophy. It tries to reach the truth by rational discussion and is itself a pattern of the disinterested research which it extols. It never bullies or deceives its reader or beguiles him with appeals to sentiment, but treats him as a fellow philosopher for whom only the truth is worth having.

This characteristic of the *Republic* forces the third criticism of Plato's programme upon our notice. Plato demanded that the philosopher should become king and impose justice upon the civilian masses, cajoling them into obedience by the "noble lie" and even by force. The seeker after truth must assert his will, and believe his opinions to be eternal truths. These demands violate the whole spirit of scientific research. The true scientist is filled with the humility which knowledge of his own ignorance brings. He knows the impossibility of reaching finality, and he recognizes the fallibility of his own reason. He cannot ape the self-certainty and presumption of practical men: nor can he call his own opinions knowledge and force them on his fellows. He cannot be the absolute dictator, as Plato demands, without turning hypothesis into dogma, and persuasion into propaganda. Socrates, the first conscientious objector to the tyranny of prejudice, could never condemn others to death for holding beliefs different from his own; and so he could never accept the arrogance of dictatorship—even dictatorship of the good. For only an unphilosophic nature can claim absolute knowledge.

The concept of the philosopher-king violates the nature of the philosopher as flagrantly as the concept of "the dictatorship of the virtuous Right" violates the facts of everyday politics. The spirit of science and philosophy stands in open contradiction to the policy which Plato advocated, and declares that Socrates must die again in the State which his disciple proposed to build. Plato set his whole hope on the dictatorship of men and women who knew the final and complete truth: but we have already seen how relative and questionable are the truths which Plato propounded and how far his conclusions were con-conditioned by traditions and instinctive impulses and the prejudices which they instigate. If a philosopher of Plato's dimensions was so liable to error and self-deception, what confidence can we have that in any State a man will be found capable of perfect knowledge? Even if he were found, can we not confidently say that he would decline every offer of supreme coercive power?

Thus the third flaw in the reasoning of the *Republic* is its suggestion that human reason is capable of infallibility and that the scientific spirit should be prepared to force others to accept it as infallible. Both these propositions are false and claim for "Reason" a position which reason must always reject. The rational man is, above all, aware of his own limitations. He knows that we are all—philosophers, politicians, priests, and ordinary folk alike—creatures of prejudice and emotion, parts in a social process greater than ourselves. He abhors the presumption that "Reason" can or should rule, and admits that his task is to analyse that which is given, to civilize the passions which are the prime motives of action and to admit the incalculability of change. Philosophy, by itself, can never discover what is right and just: it can only examine what we at any moment find right and just and point out the implications of these assumptions. For philosophy is the analysis of natural belief, and natural belief is the product of history. The philosopher who asserts that he has discovered the eternal principles of justice or government is only claiming for the beliefs of his epoch an absolute truth which does not belong to them, and trying to perpetuate something which should pass away as conditions change. And so all dogmatic philosophies, such as Platonism, become in time instruments of reaction trying vainly to explain the new epoch in terms of the old, and to torture a new society into the strait-waistcoat of an outworn code. In an era

of transition, when one social system is breaking up
to be replaced by another, the new ideas which should
grow into institutions and moral codes and political
forms are inchoate, confused, and vague. The trained
philosopher, if he accepts the established order as the
only right order, can ridicule them, expose their
inconsistency, and convince educated men and
women that they should maintain at any price the
framework of thought and life to which they are
accustomed. If he does so, he will be forced, as Plato
was forced, to destroy that freedom without which
reason must die, and with irrefutable logic he will
defend a *status quo* in which the seeds of revolution
are watered by the self-righteous opposition of the
educated classes to all forms of social change.

Plato's philosophy was an example of this type of
reasoning. Asserting the existence of absolute truth,
it succeeded in giving to a dying order and an outworn social structure the trappings of eternal verity.
It did not discover anything new, but perfected the
systematization of a current creed. For this reason it
contributed nothing to the solution of the problems
of Plato's own age. It was Aristotle, the renegade
pupil, who became the tutor of Alexander and set
his stamp upon the outlook of the Hellenistic world.

AND what of the modern Plato? We have listened
to his advice. What value do we attach to it? This
question has been partially answered in the preceding chapter. Plato to-day will fare no better than
he did two thousand years ago. Whatever his distinction as a scientist and philosopher, he will have
no lasting success as a politician, and the students
whom he has taught will fail as lamentably as their
predecessors in the Academy. For our modern Plato
is also a university teacher, a member of the class
which regards authority as its natural perquisite, and
finds it an ever more difficult task to retain that
authority in an industrial age. He is a ruler who has
renounced politics and devoted his time to research
and to the education of the men and women who
are destined for positions of influence in the councils
of the nation. Remote from practical affairs, he
lectures on the theory of politics and seeks to give
to his students a respect for reason and impartiality
and clear thinking. In discussing current affairs he
refuses to give his allegiance to any party or faction,
but regards the political scene with a sublime and
distant objectivity. But sometimes he laughingly
describes himself as a Conservative-Socialist or
Right-wing revolutionary, and sketches his ideal as
a non-party cabinet of all the talents which is strong
enough to eradicate the vices of capitalism while
suppressing all seditious movements of the Left. In
spite of his respect for tradition, he strongly depre-

cates any wild denunciation of Communist planning and admits its efficiency as an economic system and even its advantages over any other. "But," he reminds his hearers, "the advantages of a planned economy must be weighed against the horrors of the revolution which preceded it and the wickedness of that Marxism under whose banner it is being pushed forward. By all means let us introduce a planned economy, but not at the cost of our national tradition." And so he urges the formation of a non-party movement composed of intelligent and unbiased persons who see the virtues both of Socialism and of the aristocratic tradition. Such a movement will not be blinded by factional interests, since it is educated and therefore objective. It will sympathize with the lower orders since it appreciates the social evils under which they live. But it will be sure that in the end self-government for the masses will only mean the rule of demagogues: and so, in the interest of the masses, it will stop the futile party warfare and impose a sound non-party government which will bring all the benefits of Communism without its crude violence.

The modern Plato, like his ancient counterpart, has an unbounded contempt for politicians and statesmen and party leaders who are not university men. He finds politics a dirty game, and only enters them reluctantly because he knows that at the very least he and his friends are better than the present gang. Brought up in the traditions of the ruling classes, he has a natural pity for the common people whom he has learnt to know as servants, and observed from a distance at their work in the factory, at their play in the parks and holiday resorts. He has never mixed with them or spoken to them on equal terms, but has demanded and generally received a respect due to his position and superior intelligence. He knows that if they will trust him, he can give them the happiness which they crave. A man of culture, he genuinely despises the self-made industrialist and newspaper-king: with a modest professorial salary and a little private income of his own, he regards money-making as vulgar and avoids all ostentation. Industry and finance seem to him to be activities unworthy of gentlemen, although, alas, many are forced by exigencies of circumstance to take some part in them. An intellectual, he gently laughs at the superstitions of most Christians, but he attends church regularly because he sees the importance of organized religion for the maintenance of sound morality among the lower orders, and because he dislikes the scepticism and materialism of radical teachers. His genuine passions are for literature and the philosophy of science and he would gladly spend all his time in studying them. But the plight of the world compels his unwilling attention, and when he sees that human stupidity and greed are about to plunge Europe into chaos and destroy the most glorious civilization which the world has known, he feels that it is high time for men of good sense and good will to intervene and to take politics out of the hands of the plutocrats of the Right and the woolly-minded idealists of the Left. Since he and his kind are the only representatives of decency combined with intelligence, they must step down into the arena and save the masses from themselves.

The form which this salvation is to take varies from country to country. In post-war Germany the modern Plato, assuming that he must choose between the revolutionary extremes of National Socialism and Bolshevism, hesitatingly chose the former and gave it his tempered support. Holding that the Communists would destroy traditional religion and morality, and would probably prove incompetent to plan the economic system properly, he rejected the parties of the Left. The personnel of the Nazis was almost as distasteful to him; but in National Socialism he scented a return of the masses to common sense and a submission to discipline. He welcomed its stress on *Soldatentum* and its spiritual ideals, and excused its racialism as the sort of propaganda which human nature demands. Seeing clearly the weakness of the Nazi leaders, he urged his associates to be ready to take control when the Nazis had achieved power and found themselves incapable of using it. As the slump increased in severity, he was appalled at the unscrupulous use which the Nazis were making of his name and of his philosophy to justify cruelties which he had always condemned; but he was forced still to overlook them by his terror of proletarian revolution. And so he supported the counter-revolution until it occurred. Then, when the regime had been established, he approached its members with proper dignity and offered his services. He was delighted to find that he and his associates were all immediately accepted by the new leaders and put in positions of

apparent power. But he soon discovered that his
good name was being used by the politicians to further
their own designs, while they showed not the slightest
indication of accepting his advice. The evils of the
class-war still remained, but intensified by a political
and social terror: corruption had increased where
there was no opposition to expose it, and the new
national strength was being used to further a foreign
policy more imperialist than that of the democracies
which he had condemned. At first, stung by the
taunts of his fellows and associates in other lands, he
expostulated and threatened to resign. But he was
reminded that his resignation would weaken Germany
in the eyes of the world, and be an open admission of
his own failure. And so he retained his post—now a
mere sinecure—and denouncing politics as wicked,
devoted his energies to the literature and philosophy
which were his real interests.

In countries such as our own, where the social
fabric is more stable and the aristocratic tradition has
been better preserved, our modern Plato need take
no part in politics, but seeks to educate the younger
generation to the true values of the national tradition
and the true ideals of service to the community. He
calls himself a "Christian Socialist," for he is easily
able to find a form of Anglican orthodoxy com-
patible with his own philosophy. He is fond of
denouncing the evils of imperialism and the cruelties
of the industrial revolution, and he paints a noble
picture of an eighteenth century when reason ruled
and England prospered. A superb stylist—nicknamed
the second Burke—he is already famous for his

Reflections on the Russian Revolution and his new pamphlet on the Communist menace in Spain is remarkable for its special word of commendation to the Catholic Church on its support of the anti-Reds in their noble crusade against atheism. Ruthless in his condemnation of Fascist cruelty, he nevertheless reminds his readers that we must be realists, not romantics, and that in politics our objective study of right must not be disturbed by a sympathy—proper in its place—for the oppressed. Since therefore the civilized countries must at all costs unite to put down the menace of class-war, he urges us to welcome Fascism abroad and to seek to bring it to reason by courtesy and by fair offers of redress for injustice. For Fascism is only the attempt to accomplish by force that discipline of the masses which our peaceful tradition has effected, and with time and patience it can be schooled to be a faithful ally in the salvation of European civilization from class-war and from the Yellow Peril.

His chief interest to-day is foreign policy. Here he writes and teaches of the urgent need for co-operation between the nations of Europe and for the strengthening of the League of Nations by the inclusion in it of all civilized nations. With his deep appreciation of our Western culture he views with apprehension the Japanese expansion and sometimes speaks of Russia as an Oriental State with a veneer of Western culture. On all suitable occasions he exhorts Europe to stand together against a common foe and to break down the barriers between nations linked by a common culture.

In home affairs he sympathizes with those progressive Conservatives who preach a tempered State-Socialism and desire to give the workers all that they really need, while resolutely denouncing all Socialist and Communist agitators. Deeply distressed by the collapse of organized religion, and by the growth of vulgarity in literature, drama, and architecture, he tries to imbue his younger friends with a philosophical spirit resolutely opposed to scepticism, and to inspire them to reconstruct Christian theology upon a sound philosophical basis, and to reconcile it with science. Unemployment and war he regards as necessary evils which can only be cured by elevating the tone of statesmanship in all countries so that the policy of every nation shall be determined not by self-interest, but by respect for law. Until the time, he often says, when the intelligent and the independent mind replaces the professional politician and agitator, the world will know no cessation from its evils. Meanwhile we must be thankful for the benefits which Providence has bestowed upon us and be constantly on our guard to preserve our political tradition from further deterioration, and to ensure that "the gentleman" is still the type of English honour. And always if sudden disaster looms up and the class-war is blown into flame, all those who care for England must be prepared to save the country from mob-violence and irresponsible agitators. Then when order has been restored, men of good will must see to it that no undue victimization occurs, and that that measure of reform is pushed through which will give to the lower orders their just portion of the benefits of life.

Stripped of the brilliance of the Platonic style and its wealth of imagery, the modern programme sounds dull and a little sententious, the proposals of a thinker strangely out of touch with the movements of history and with the thoughts and passions of everyday life. This is as it should be. Plato *was* out of touch with any but the narrow circle of Greek intellectuals which we often identify with ancient Greece. He had never known the time when Pericles bridged the gap between the aristocrat and the plebeian, between the intellectual and the business man, and thus forged a real community which gave to every class and to every individual a living sense of their integration in the social order. In his lifetime class division and specialization of interest had torn the close-knit fabric of the city-state and atomized its collective spirit. So, too, the modern Plato has little knowledge of the community in which he lives. He believes that the educated gentlemen with whom he associates are the only people in the land with a genuine sense of social responsibility and a true feeling for the English tradition. For him the Public School is the central fact of our social life. Belonging to the academic world, he knows little of things outside its quiet walls. Steeped in its high traditions of integrity and intellectual accuracy, he views with disgust the shoddiness of the practical man's thought, the commercialism of his motives, and the blatant contradictions in the policies which he adopts. He is critical of university life, but at least he sees in it an order and a rationality which can be moulded into proper shape. But the outside world seems to him a hopeless bedlam of stupidity, pettiness, and greed.

And yet he cannot renounce it completely. Many of the students whom he teaches are destined for commanding positions in industry, in politics, and in the administration. Wherever he turns his eyes he finds the university man in authority, and often enough a cabinet minister or the editor of a great newspaper is his week-end guest. He is aware that the British university is—as the ancient Plato had desired—the pedagogue of practical life and through its unpolitical activities is shaping the policies of an empire. The Academy is the brain of the body politic, and through it the old aristocratic regime has been transformed into an aristocracy of educated men. He is therefore indirectly but vitally responsible for the government of his country. His philosophy is the framework of national policy, his morality is recognizable in the actions of its statesmen. Why then, he asks himself, does the world seem to be heading for destruction? Why are his students when they return to practical affairs unable to impose upon them the reasoned order of university life and university thought? Uneasily, he feels that Platonic education, though it can school young men to think rationally, cannot teach them to apply that reason in the outside world. It can produce political philosophers: but it cannot produce philosopher-kings.

And so in the tranquillity of the university Plato is ill at ease and labours unceasingly to elaborate a political and social theory, schooled in whose discipline the student can go out to kill the dragons of stupidity and greed. But because the university is part of the established order, and because the philosophy which he teaches is a philosophy of that order, Plato, the spiritual revolutionary, remains the apologist of the *status quo*, and the new *Republic* is as sterile as the old. It is rational and filled with noble sentiments, but it is rooted in the past—the sublime philosophy of a lost cause.

For this reason Plato is always "respectable." His revolutionary proposals—a *via media* between re-action and proletarian revolution—are carefully pondered by the powers that be. His week-end guests return to work invigorated by his idealism, determined to furbish up the old system and eradicate its evils; even crusted Tories admit that, if the Left would only take Plato's advice, they would sweep the country. The Churches regard him as a Socialist who softens the waters of revolution with sweet reason, and the League of Nations Union claims him as the most distinguished member of the Com-mittee for Intellectual Co-operation. Trusted and honoured by all who matter, he is recognized as the most wholesome influence in British politics, a "genuine idealist who remains a gentleman even when he preaches revolution."

And yet Plato's revolution is never achieved. In spite of his reputation and in spite of the influence of his pupils, his ideals are never realized, though always admired. The order and reason of the university stand in horrid contrast to the anarchy outside. Fascism and Communism are untouched by his persuasions: unemployment remains; and the comity of European nations for which he yearns is split by ever-growing fissures. Unheedful of the calm advice of established reason, the world rumbles towards catastrophe. Neither Plato nor his pupils—despite their commanding positions and their gentlemanly ideals—can do anything to prevent it.

Socrates cannot prevent it either. But at least he knows that he does not know. He does not sit in academic tranquillity teaching young men how to think and rule: instead, he goes out into the every-day world and mixes with all sorts of people, seeking to know human nature before he condemns it. He offers no programme of spiritual revolution, and produces no students with clear-cut philosophies of life who can say precisely what truth and justice are. He tries not to establish a new authority, but to disrupt prejudice wherever he finds it—even in the university. The conscientious objector to prejudice and intellectual presumption, he condemns the new Plato and the new *Republic* as heartily as he condemns any other dogmatism which ossifies the free spirit of reason and perverts it into an instrument of oppression.

A FRIENDLY critic, who read the proofs of the foregoing pages, complained that they were entirely negative in character. "What you have done," he said, "is to expound Plato's case against Greek democracy and then to show that his own counter-proposals were completely ineffective. After that you turned to the modern world and repeated the procedure. You allowed Plato to criticize democracy and Fascism and Communism, and then you went on to pour cold water on all his positive philosophy. So far, so good; but what conclusion is your reader meant to come to? Where do you yourself stand?" To these questions I shall try to give some answer in this chapter.

In what I have so far written, I have tried to suppress my own views and to translate Plato's political philosophy into modern terms. In so doing I have found myself in the position of an *advocatus diaboli* working out a case for dictatorship more convincing than that of most Fascist apologists whom I have read. The result will, I fear, shock many readers of Plato. They will be unwilling to accept the picture which I have presented, and will urge that it is a caricature, not a portrait, of the Plato whom they admire. There are two comments to be made upon this criticism. In the first place great philosophers have often been bad political and social critics. The political influence of Hegel, for instance, was disastrous, and it is rare to find men like Aristotle and Hume who combined profound philosophical insight with an eye for practical affairs. There is a danger that, out of respect for his eminence as a metaphysician, we should swallow Plato's political opinions too easily, and it was partly to meet this danger that *Plato To-day* was written. In the second place, I should not myself agree that the views I have attributed to the modern Plato are either negligible or absurd. On the contrary, the criticisms which he has made of democracy and communism (the germs of which may all be found in the *Republic*) seem to me very difficult to contravert. The reader may *feel* that Plato must be wrong; but he will not find it easy to build a case for democracy, either in the Liberal or in the Marxian sense of that word, which will withstand Plato's analysis.

My answer then to my friendly critic is this: "I am a democrat and a Socialist who sees Fascism rejected and democracy defended on quite inadequate grounds; and it is because I realize that our greatest danger to-day is not the easy acceptance but the easy rejection of Totalitarian philosophy, that I have tried to restate the *Republic* in modern terms."

It is a sound political principle not to underrate your opponent, and in this book I have tried to make him as formidable as possible, and to expose the weakness of much so-called democratic theory. If the reader gets an uneasy feeling that he cannot contravert Plato's arguments, I shall be well content. For in that case he will have begun to see that the real menace of Fascism is due to the scarcity of democrats with a practical and realistic creed. Dictatorships do not arise merely owing to the folly of

foreigners. They are imposed firstly because democratic institutions become unmanageable and awkward
for the ruling interests, and secondly *because the
common man does not find democracy worth defending*.
The success of Fascism in the international field is due
largely to the "pacifism" of Great Britain. This
"pacifism" in its turn is the result of a profound
scepticism about the value of democracy and of the
League of Nations. The ordinary Englishman is not
at the present moment prepared to die for anything
really important, least of all for democracy. And our
statesmen seem to agree with him. It is difficult to
name one principle or obligation or imperial interest
which they will not sacrifice to avoid war.

Democracy, in fact, has lost belief in itself, and
become an inert instead of a dynamic force in world
affairs. Fascism has the initiative; and we are content
to sneer at its philosophy while we concede to its
statesmen one vital interest after another. This collapse
of morale is partly due to our own self-ignorance.
Unlike our opponents, we are uncertain what the
democracy is for which we stand. Our paeans to
freedom and justice and peace are empty formulae
which hide a horrid doubt in our own minds, and our
philosophy has become little better than an apology
for concessions extorted from us by force of circumstance. Whatever we do we dub "democratic" and
hope thereby to hide our dishonour from ourselves.
The sacrifice of Abyssinia is excused on grounds of
procedure, that of Spain on the score of preventing
world-war.

The trouble about most defenders of democracy is

that their theory is so different from their practice. They paint a picture of a country where the people is sovereign and where all men are equal before the law and then they equate this millennial vision with contemporary England. Is it surprising that the man in the street begins to doubt the sincerity of politicians and publicists who constantly assure him that he is already in the Kingdom of Heaven? Is it astonishing that he says, "Well, if *this* is equality and liberty and justice, I don't think much of them"? The League of Nations was killed by the enthusiasts who mistook a clumsy instrument of justice for justice itself. Democracy is on the way to meeting the same fate.

The first positive lesson, then, which Plato can teach us is that to defend democracy we must be as realistic as its opponents. We must be able to see things as they are, and to distinguish *ideal* and *fact*; we must be willing to criticize the existing order as ruthlessly as they; we must not only have fine ideals, but count up the cost of realizing them and recognize what changes they will undergo in the process of realization. Above all we must not over-estimate the nature of human beings, but learn from the Platos of this world just so much: that the ordinary man accepts comfort and security without worrying where they come from; that a Government's first job is to govern and only in the second place to govern well; that morality by itself can never outweigh interest; that justice is impossible unless there is power to enforce it; and lastly that political institutions are totally insignificant in comparison with social tradition and economic organization.

To defend democracy, in fact, we must accept a great deal, both of Plato's criticism of democratic theory, and of his analysis of our present democratic institutions. But this is not enough. In the second place we must make up our minds *precisely* where his philosophy fails. True democracy is un-Platonic, because it springs from the Christian notion of personality; and it is only if we believe in this notion that we can refute Plato and show that his philosophy has no sufficient message for the modern world. If this is true, it should come as a shock to discover how well Plato's philosophy is adapted to our "Christian" ways of thought—most of our Christian theory and practice is indistinguishable from it. For this reason, as the true democrat must start with the assumption that the world has still to be made democratic, so the Christian must assume that it is still pagan, despite the existence of "democratic" institutions and "Christian" churches. Only a revolutionary democracy and a revolutionary Christianity can hope to prevail to-day. Institutionalism will kill them both, if it gets the chance, and turn them into "noble lies" which modern Platonists can use to defend the *status quo*.

For fundamentally both are the assertions of *incredibles*. Against the realism of those who accept the existing order and seek to maintain it, they preach an impossibility and try to make it come true. The true democrat and the true Christian admit the Platonic analysis of man as he is, but they know that they can change him by their faith in man as he ought to be. It was this faith which Plato lacked, as I have tried to show in the concluding pages of the chapter on Communism. He felt himself to be a member of a dying order in which the good was only a survival from a previous golden age; and so his philosophy and his political career were devoted to the defence of dying values against the corrosion of history. Truth and justice on his view must be rescued by an *élite*. The sphere of freedom must be contracted until it includes only those few elect spirits who are worthy of it.

A real democratic philosophy will be resolutely opposed to such an outlook. It cannot be content to defend a social order by the maintenance of an authoritarian tradition: on the contrary, it must be resolved to expand the sphere of freedom and, with this ideal in view, to take such practical measures as are necessary to enable every citizen to become a member of the *élite*. Seeing the pettiness and spiritual poverty of the "civilian" as clearly as Plato, it must ask "what is the cause of this pettiness and spiritual poverty? Are they intrinsic or are they resultants of a particular social and economic order?" Admitting the plight of human nature, it will still assert its infinite *possibilities* and will be prepared so to change the present order that these possibilities can become actualities. For the democratic faith is not tied to any political or social system. It regards all systems (including "democracy") as instruments for the self-realization of human nature; and if representative institutions are shown to be no longer useful for that purpose then the democrat must look elsewhere for other instruments and better institutions.

The modern democrat too often confounds parliamentary government with democracy, and assumes that every critic of the one must necessarily be an enemy of the other. He forgets that parliaments were forged for specific purposes under specific historical conditions, and that the instruments of freedom can become, under changed conditions, the instruments of oligarchy. And so he fails to realize that a defence of parliamentary government as such may, in certain circumstances, be completely undemocratic. History is constantly putting new wine into old bottles.

The faith of democracy, therefore, can never be expressed in the *defence* of anything. You cannot *defend* democracy against Fascism, and if you try to, you will find yourself supporting your enemy unawares. Democracy (because it is founded upon the infinite possibilities of human nature) must always be on the attack, always on the side of social change against the forces of "law and order," always critical of established institutions and social codes. It knows that, without the dynamic of its faith, human society will fall back into oligarchy and injustice. Where faith in the impossible dies, Plato's estimate of human nature becomes correct.

But democracy is not a mere ideal, mystically envisaged by a few dreamers; for the belief in the infinite value of human *personality* is also the belief in human *reason*, and at this point the ideal of Jesus is fused with that of Socrates. I have tried to show how Plato, in his attempt to re-establish a Greek aristocratic order, departed further and further from the principles of his master, until he turned the Socratic belief in reason into a dogmatic and authoritarian code. But democracy, just as it is tied to no particular institution, is tied to no eternal philosophy. Democratic thought must always remain a searching for truth and the democrat can never cease to be the man who knows that he knows nothing. He must regard all ready-made systems with suspicion: he must reject self-evident formulae and "first principles" outright. For he is aware of the all-inclusive nature of the historical process of which he is a part, and he knows that the dominant classes will and must build themselves rational structures with which to defend their economic and social supremacy. Most men and all societies are naturally conservative: they try to deny change and to maintain ways of thought and action when they are no longer socially useful. For this reason human intellect is chiefly used to justify inertia, and to extol as knowledge what is already prejudice. The Socratic search for truth is the principle which seeks to undermine this dogmatism of inertia, to break down the rational defences of prejudice, and so to allow human personality to grow and to adapt itself to new conditions. Denying that any system of theology or ethics or law or government can be eternally valid, it appeals against Reason to reason itself, against this system of justice to justice, against these laws to law.

This appeal to the common sense and to the critical faculty of the ordinary man against the formidable structures of established orthodoxy is the vital force of democratic philosophy. On the one hand it displays a deep humility—for it admits its own inability to formulate an eternal truth. On the other it proudly challenges the infallibility of all the promulgators of Reason and denies that they are an *élite* endowed with superior powers. Its innate humility is therefore the deadliest enemy of absolutism in all forms. Its simple assertion that all men are equal in their ignorance of the final values is the dissolvent of vested interests in knowledge and in social power.

The attack of democratic reason upon absolutism has taken different forms in different epochs. Socrates was compelled by his creed to attack Athenian democracy, Jesus to expose the Pharisees. In our own era the doctrines of natural right and social contract were in the first place weapons for the destruction of authoritarian Governments and Churches. Then in their turn they became the philosophical bulwarks of a new bourgeois social system, and Marxism took their place as the instrument of social criticism. The democratic spirit, directly its ideas become accepted and established, is forced to escape from them and to find other and newer concepts with which to fulfil its task as the "gadfly" of human lethargy.

The crisis of the modern world is at bottom caused by the failure of this democratic spirit to find a new basis for its attack on dogma. Our world is breaking up; but we remain supporters of one or other of the established forms—adherents of status not of equality. The Fascism which confronts us is the self-conscious refusal of the powers-that-be to face the necessity of change; and it has drawn to itself a pseudo-revolutionary enthusiasm, merely because the democratic spirit, becoming institutionalized, has lost its forward drive.

This fact is glaringly obvious if we examine the political Left in our own country. Much of its organization and philosophy is wellnigh as conservative as that of its opponents. Its early missionary zeal is gone; its thought has settled down into well-worn dogmatic channels. Instead of uniting the discontented and the oppressed by the fervour of its message, it is too often content to defend what privileges its supporters possess, and to purge itself of heresies and of unorthodox zealots. Left and Right to-day are alike social institutions, part and parcel of the existing order, living alongside one another and scratching each other occasionally according to the polite ceremonies of parliamentary procedure. The same holds true of the trade unions and the Co-operative movement, and above all, of the Churches. They, too, have settled down to fulfil their appointed functions in the *status quo*.

This institutionalism is mirrored in the thought of many so-called Radicals. For the most part Socialist analysis has become scholastic, a studious development of a received body of doctrine which grows ever more academic and more remote from the current problems of society. The result of this loss of social dynamic is twofold. On the one hand, the Conservative forces, robbed of the healthy impact of Radical criticism, are completely immobile, and on the other, the few men and women who still feel the spirit of democracy find no corporate body in which they can play their part. Unable to co-operate in the work of social emancipation, isolated and bitter in their enforced inactivity, they become anarchic and egocentric prophets, or, retiring from the social struggle, relapse into aesthetic or mystical dilettantism. Like Socrates, they find no ground where their seed can grow, and so their criticism, which should stimulate a healthy movement of change, only goes to accelerate the process of social disintegration.

Such is the state of modern democracy in which Fascism is bound to grow. It can be cured only if we become urgently aware of the imminence of the catastrophe, and if, holding fast to our denial of the infallibility of established dogma, and believing still in the infinite possibilities latent in human nature, we try to awaken once more that spirit of conscientious objection to prejudice and to Phariseeism of which Socrates was the first example. Only when Western civilization has shaken off the shackles of the past and created a new social order worthy of the human dignity of the common man, will democracy and religion be once more realized in human society. Till then both must remain faiths, filled with a prophetic anger at the sight of the nations and societies which use their name in vain, and, because they are grounded in the heart of the common man, powerful enough to remove mountains.

It is Socrates, not Plato, whom we need.

BIBLIOGRAPHY

ON the subject with which this book is concerned—the influence of Platonic philosophy upon practical politics—very little has been written. However, for the general reader who may wish to study the problems I have raised a little more deeply, I append a list of books which should be of use, though many of them do not bear directly upon the subject.

CHAPTERS 1-4

There is no really good history of Greece available to English readers; Mitchell and Caspari's one-volume edition of *Grote* is still the best work on the subject; and Naomi Mitchison's *Cloud Cuckoo Land* gives a more vivid impression than many learned volumes. The *Legacy of Greece*, the *Pageant of Greece* by Sir Richard Livingstone, and Sir Alfred Zimmern's *Greek Commonwealth* are all worth reading; but anyone who really wants to understand the background of Plato's thought cannot do better than to read *Thucydides* himself in the Everyman translation and the *Epistles of Plato*.

Out of the mass of books on Plato and Socrates I should recommend in the first place Professor Taylor's *Life of Socrates*, Professor Barker's *Political Thought of Plato and Aristotle*, and *Plato's Thought*, by G. M. A. Grube. These are all useful introductions, but for the keen student Grote's *Plato and Other Companions of Socrates* remains far the most stimulating work on the subject. Second to it I should put the Oxford translation of Aristotle's *Politics*. Though much of it must be obscure to the inexpert reader, no one can fail to enjoy reading the most downright and realistic critic of Platonism.

Unfortunately, there are few good translations of Plato available, but Lindsay's *Republic* is an exception to this rule. Jowett must be relied on for most of the other Dialogues, but the reader is warned that his smooth and pseudo-archaic style gives a false impression of the original, besides being often grossly inaccurate.

For the remaining chapters I have compiled a rather haphazard book list. It is by no means comprehensive, but it will at least indicate whence many of my ideas are derived.

CHAPTERS 5–6

Walter Bagehot: *The English Constitution.*
R. L. Nettleship: *Theory of Education in Plato's Republic.*
R. H. Tawney: *Equality.*
H. J. Laski: *Rise of European Liberalism.*
Graham Wallas: *Human Nature in Politics.*
Walter Lippmann: *Public Opinion.*

CHAPTER 8

Edmund Burke: *French Revolution.*
Thomas Paine: *Rights of Man.*
John MacMurray: *Philosophy of Communism*; *Creative Society.*
W. H. Chamberlin: *Russia's Iron Age.*
John Strachey: *Theory and Practice of Socialism.*
S. Hooke: *Towards an Understanding of Karl Marx.*
H. J. Laski: *The State in Theory and Practice.*
Arthur Rosenberg: *History of Bolshevism.*

CHAPTER 9

Adolf Hitler: *Mein Kampf* (German edition only).
Arthur Rosenberg: *Myths of Twentieth Century.*
Bernard Bosanquet: *Philosophical Theory of the State.*

CHAPTER 10

E. Meyer: *Geschichte des Altertums* (Vol. v).

CHAPTERS 11–12

A. Niebuhr: *Moral Man and Immoral Society*; *Interpretation of Christian Ethics.*